TRUMAN CAPOTE

MODERN LITERATURE SERIES

GENERAL EDITOR: PHILIP WINSOR

In the same series:

S. Y. AGNON   *Harold Fisch*
SHERWOOD ANDERSON   *Welford Dunaway Taylor*
LEONID ANDREYEV   *Josephine M. Newcombe*
ISAAC BABEL   *R. W. Hallett*
SIMONE DE BEAUVOIR   *Robert Cottrell*
SAUL BELLOW   *Brigitte Scheer-Schäzler*
BERTOLT BRECHT   *Willy Haas*
JORGE LUIS BORGES   *George R. McMurray*
ALBERT CAMUS   *Carol Petersen*
TRUMAN CAPOTE   *Helen S. Garson*
WILLA CATHER   *Dorothy Tuck McFarland*
JOHN CHEEVER   *Samuel T. Coale*
COLETTE   *Robert Cottrell*
JOSEPH CONRAD   *Martin Tucker*
JULIO CORTÁZAR   *Evelyn Picon Garfield*
JOHN DOS PASSOS   *George J. Becker*
THEODORE DREISER   *James Lundquist*
FRIEDRICH DÜRRENMATT   *Armin Arnold*
T. S. ELIOT   *Joachim Seyppel*
WILLIAM FAULKNER   *Joachim Seyppel*
F. SCOTT FITZGERALD   *Rose Adrienne Gallo*
FORD MADOX FORD   *Sondra J. Stang*
JOHN FOWLES   *Barry N. Olshen*
MAX FRISCH   *Carol Petersen*
ROBERT FROST   *Elaine Barry*
GABRIEL GARCÍA MÁRQUEZ   *George R. McMurray*
MAKSIM GORKI   *Gerhard Habermann*
GÜNTER GRASS   *Kurt Lothar Tank*
ROBERT GRAVES   *Katherine Snipes*
PETER HANDKE   *Nicholas Hern*
LILLIAN HELLMAN   *Doris V. Falk*
ERNEST HEMINGWAY   *Samuel Shaw*
HERMANN HESSE   *Franz Baumer*
CHESTER HIMES   *James Lundquist*
HUGO VON HOFMANNSTHAL   *Lowell W. Bangerter*
UWE JOHNSON   *Mark Boulby*
JAMES JOYCE   *Armin Arnold*
FRANZ KAFKA   *Franz Baumer*
RING LARDNER   *Elizabeth Evans*
D. H. LAWRENCE   *George T. Becker*
SINCLAIR LEWIS   *James Lundquist*
GEORG LUKÁCS   *Ehrhard Bahr and Ruth Goldschmidt Kunzer*
NORMAN MAILER   *Philip H. Bufithis*
BERNARD MALAMUD   *Sheldon J. Hershinow*

(continued on last page of book)

TRUMAN CAPOTE

Helen S. Garson

WITH HALFTONE ILLUSTRATIONS

FREDERICK UNGAR PUBLISHING CO.
NEW YORK

80-35011

For My Mother

Library of Congress Cataloging in Publication Data

Garson, Helen S
    Truman Capote.

    (Modern literature monographs)
    Bibliography: p.
    Includes index.
    1.   Capote, Truman, 1924–   —Criticism
and interpretation.
PS3505.A59Z655   813'.54   80–5336
ISBN 0–8044–2229–X
ISBN 0–8044–6172–4 (pbk.)

Contents

1   The Many Faces of Truman Capote:
The Man and the Work   1

2   The Lost Child: *Other Voices, Other Rooms*   13

3   The Unexplored Realm: *A Tree of Night
and Other Stories*   27

4   Paths of Memory: *The Grass Harp*   63

5   Never Love a Wild Thing:
Breakfast at Tiffany's   79

6   Surprised by Joy: Stories of the
Fifties and Sixties   91

7   People, Places, and the Celebrity Life:
The Nonfiction Pieces   111

8   Acts of Darkness: *In Cold Blood*   141

9   The Unforgivable Sin: *Answered Prayers*   165

Notes   187
Bibliography   195
Index   201
    Pictures appear between pages 62 and 63.

1

The Many Faces
of Truman Capote:
The Man and the Work

Truman Capote has been in the public eye for more
than thirty years. Everyone knows his name, if not his
work, for he has been interviewed, quoted, and photo-
graphed regularly. A traveler at an airport newsstand
buys *Esquire* or *Playboy* and finds something by or
about Capote; a woman leafing through *Mademoiselle*
or *Vogue* turns to a Capote short story, perhaps a
reprint of a work from the early days, a reader of a
current study of the American media sees Capote
comments or comments about Capote; [1] the television
viewer watches him on talk shows; and the student
finds the novels on a course syllabus.

With all the publicity surrounding Capote, one
may lose sight of the fact that the writer and the "star"
are not the same. Perhaps the decline of his work in
the past decade results from Capote's failure to recognize the differences.

Capote's career reached its summit when his
much heralded book, *In Cold Blood*, was published.
Because of the widespread interest as well as the
enormous financial success of the book, reviewers
spoke of 1966 as belonging to Capote. The work
brought the kind of acclaim that many people had
anticipated for him since his wunderkind years when
his first stories were printed in various magazines.

The early years of his life provided the substance

for the future novelist. Born in New Orleans, September 30, 1924, to Nina and Joseph Persons, Truman was their only child. It was an unhappy marriage—Capote has stated that his mother married only to escape from her hometown, Monroeville [2]—and his parents were divorced when he was four.

Capote's mother went to New York, leaving him behind with her family, the Faulks, in rural Alabama. Although she remarried, she didn't send for her son until he was "ten or so" [3] and she knew she wasn't going to bear any more children.

During those years in Monroeville, Capote was a very lonely little boy, always feeling different from others. His only friends were some black children (those were the years of separation and segregation), and Harper Lee, who later gained renown for her novel, *To Kill a Mockingbird*. Dearest to him, however, was an elderly cousin, Miss Sook Faulk, a childlike, simple woman, who was wise about many things a small boy could share. Capote has said that "A Christmas Memory" and "The Thanksgiving Visitor" were written about her; it is apparent that *The Grass Harp* was also. Many readers prefer these tender stories to anything else Capote has written. But some critics favor the psychological-supernatural stories [4] that had a similar origin in his boyhood experiences as well as in the imagination that was stirred by tales of terror he heard and told.

Because of Capote's dark stories, and his first published novel, *Other Voices, Other Rooms*, people have always associated his work with the tradition of Southern gothicism. In spite of his obvious links to that literature, Capote does not like to be categorized as a Southern writer, and he points out that he left Alabama as a child.

When the boy moved to New York, he was adopted by Joseph Capote, Nina Faulk Persons' sec-

ond husband, and Truman then took his surname.
While his mother and stepfather lived in New York,
he attended private schools there for a few years, first
Trinity, and then a military boarding school, St. John's
Academy. Later he went to a public high school in
Greenwich, Connecticut, where his parents had
moved. In high school, he was befriended by a teacher
named Catharine Wood, to whom he dedicated the
first edition (1956) of "A Christmas Memory." By the
time he got to high school he had been writing for a
number of years, and he started sending stories
around for publication when he was about fifteen.

But he was unhappy in school, and at seventeen
he dropped out. After working briefly at odd jobs, he
returned to New York.

Capote went to work for *The New Yorker* magazine, but not as a writer. He started out in the ac-
counting department, was transferred to the art department where he catalogued cartoons and clipped
newspapers, and then was moved up to write items
for the column "The Talk of the Town." At the same
time he was working as a freelancer, reading movie
scripts and writing anecdotes for a digest publication.

He spent his nights on his stories, writing in pencil on lined pages, a custom he still follows. When he
was seventeen he had his first stories accepted for
publication—three, all on the same day. Then, at the
age of nineteen, he won the O'Henry Prize for the
short story, "Miriam." He was convinced that he was
going to be famous.

After two years at *The New Yorker*, Capote left.
In different essays and interviews he has given various
reasons for that step. One is that the poet Robert
Frost took a dislike to him and had him fired by
writing a calumnious letter to Harold Ross, the editor
of the magazine. Another is that after the publication
of "Miriam" he signed a contract with Random House

and was given an advance which enabled him to
spend all his time on his own writing. The third is
that he had begun his first novel, *Summer Crossing,*
and wanted to finish it.[6]

Capote went to stay with relatives in Alabama,
in the isolated little country town that was to serve
as the model for Noon City in *Other Voices, Other
Rooms.* Soon, however, he became increasingly dis-
satisfied with *Summer Crossing.* One winter day as
he was walking in the woods near a creek, he came
to an abandoned mill that he remembered from his
childhood. As a boy he had often gone swimming in
the creek with Harper Lee, the girl "who was the
counterpart of Idabel" in *Other Voices, Other Rooms.*
And he remembered being bitten by a cottonmouth
moccasin. One boyhood memory after another came
crowding in. Thus, the story that was to be the new
novel came to him. Filled with great excitement, he
returned to the farmhouse, went to his room, put
away his first attempt at a novel, the manuscript of
which has since been lost, and began to work on
Other Voices, Other Rooms.

Because his writing routine was upsetting to his
relatives, Capote left. He bought a Greyhound bus
ticket and headed for New Orleans, which was his
hometown and a city that he knew well from boyhood
summers when he returned to the South to visit
family.

During one summer in New Orleans, Capote had
met two men who were to become the models for cousin Randolph in the novel. One was a retired captain
of a fishing trawler, a man who lived with his sister.
The captain, an asthmatic, smoked medicinal ciga-
rettes, designed and sewed beautiful tapestrylike pictures, and spent his days in a darkened room. The
other person, Randolph's "spiritual ancestor," was a
plump, blonde man who sat alone in the corner of a

cafe, drawing pictures of people who came there. The young Capote would listen to the artist, "a monologist obsessed with death, betrayed passion, and unfulfilled talent." Both men became linked with the writer's early memories and consequently became part of the novel.

On his arrival in New Orleans Capote rented a room in the French Quarter. There he wrote half the story, living lonely, carefully scheduled days and nights, never getting in touch with friends. Once, by accident, he saw his father. Years later, Capote wrote of the irony of the meeting, "considering that though I was unaware of it at the time, the central theme of *Other Voices, Other Rooms* was my search for the existence of this essentially imaginary person."

Capote left New Orleans and went on to North Carolina, Saratoga Springs, New York, and finally to Nantucket, where at last he completed the novel. It had taken him two years to write the book which made him a celebrity at the age of twenty-four.

Although Capote became famous almost overnight, his novel was rejected by some because of the homosexual theme, or the gothicism and the grotesque characters; others faulted it for what they called a concentration of art over life. One critic spoke for a number of scholars when he wrote that Capote lacked both taste and judgment and, further, that neither time nor experience would change those deficiencies.[7] However, the public stood on the side which found the book exciting, one of the most absorbing in years. And they read it.

Part of the attention given the new novel came from Capote's early understanding of the impact of publicity. Throughout his career, he has been able to keep his name and photograph current. Even before the publication of *Other Voices, Other Rooms,* Capote's picture was featured in *Life,* in an article about

promising young writers.[8] But the photograph which
is unforgettable even now is the one on the book
jacket of *Other Voices, Other Rooms:* a beautiful,
young, blonde Capote reclines on an elegant couch
and gazes into the reader's eyes provocatively. Today
that photograph is as well known as the book, as we
are reminded in the November 1979 issue of *Vogue,*
which has a portrait of the fifty-five-year-old Capote
humorously striking the same pose. Yet Capote is
scornful of those who suggest the book became a best-
seller because of the cover. He observes that he had
been writing for fourteen years before the publication
of the novel; he was no beginner.[9]

The inventive use of public relations through frequent interviews and release of photographs has been
responsible for much of Capote's renown, but it has
also led to an adverse response from a number of
literary reviewers, who often have refused to consider his work noteworthy. Only when *In Cold Blood*
was published did Capote receive attention from all
the critics. A decade after its publication, both American and European scholars continue to write about
the seminal import of the book. Even so, there still
remains the ingrained view, particularly in some parts
of academia, that Capote is a minor commercial
writer.[10]

Not surprisingly, Capote views academic people
as dull, gray, and noncreative. Inasmuch as he has
produced a number of works that continue to be read,
studied, and discussed, he must be regarded as one
of the more significant writers of the second half of
this century. Undoubtedly, *Other Voices, Other
Rooms, A Tree of Night and Other Stories, Breakfast
at Tiffany's,* and *In Cold Blood,* his best works, will
have reader appeal for a very long time and will remain influential for other writers.

Some reviewers criticized Capote's fiction prior to

In Cold Blood for its unrealistic characters, fanciful plots, and its indifference to moral and societal issues. Still, there are critics who find those same qualities praiseworthy, commenting that Capote's stories develop from the historical conventions of the romance. They refer to Richard Chase's discussion of the particularities of the romance in *The American Novel and Its Tradition*. Chase writes that the romance does not observe "ordinary novelistic requirements of verisimilitude, development, and continuity." It has a "freedom . . . from the conditions of actuality." The characters may be "two-dimensional," the plot "highly colored," and the episodes implausible and "astonishing." [11]

Readers who accept the idea that Capote's early writing should be categorized as romance can then dismiss irrelevant issues. They are the people who find Capote's second book remarkable in its voyage into the human psyche via the route of the romance. *A Tree of Night and Other Stories* is like a heavily woven tapestry of different depths that draws one from layer to layer. The collection contains stories in both a light and dark mode. Although Capote was never again to publish stories of the latter kind, some of the characteristics appear in other works, and some of the characters surface under other names in the fiction of the past decade.

Capote has spoken of his work as belonging to cycles in his development as a writer. He labels *Other Voices, Other Rooms* as the end of the first cycle, and he places *A Tree of Night and Other Stories* in the second. During the ten-year period of his second cycle, his most varied and prolific, he wrote the autobiographical story, "A Christmas Memory"; *The Grass Harp,* a novel which he also turned into a play; "House of Flowers," a short story which later became a musical comedy; essays and portraits, *Local Color* and *Ob-*

servations; film scripts for *Beat the Devil* and *The Innocents;* a nonfiction, comic, book-length travel report, *The Muses Are Heard;* and finally, the very popular novel, *Breakfast at Tiffany's.*

Capote's third cycle, corresponding to the decade of the sixties, was devoted primarily to the preparation and writing of *In Cold Blood,* although during that time he also published two of his well-known pieces, "A Thanksgiving Visitor," which is a spin-off from "A Christmas Memory," and "Among the Paths to Eden," one of his best short stories, and one which led some critics to predict, incorrectly, that this was the direction his future fiction was to follow.

Much has been written about *In Cold Blood,* its genre, its style, its narrator. Every conceivable type of study of the book has been undertaken. In interviews Capote continues to explain the genesis of the book and his interest in developing a new art form. During the time that he was writing articles on a regular basis for *The New Yorker,* particularly those that became *The Muses Are Heard,* he developed a strong interest in narrative journalism. He decided he wanted to expand reporting into something more meaningful, to create a work which combined journalism and fiction. When his attention was piqued by a news story of the murder of a Kansas family, he felt that he had found the subject matter to experiment with a different type of novel. The result was Capote's most noted book and greatest literary achievement, to which he gave the designation, the "nonfiction novel." Other writers, American and European, have been using similar techniques since Capote introduced them; yet, he is bitter about the failure of some critics to acknowledge his contribution in devising a new theory of writing. One of those he singles out is Norman Mailer, who, Capote says, was disparaging of the form, yet quickly saw the value of it for his own

work and wrote a number of nonfiction novels.[12]
Whether or not sufficient credit is given to Capote for
his innovativeness, nobody can question the impact
the book has had.

Between the publication of *In Cold Blood* and
1975, Capote wrote comparatively little. Much of his
time was spent making public appearances, or social-
izing. In great demand everywhere, he himself gave
the definitive party of the decade, a black-and-white
dress ball for the rich and the famous, the Beautiful
People and the powerful people.

Capote gave his party in an attempt to ward off
the great sadness that had come over him after the
completion of *In Cold Blood.* He is a man who suffers
from frequent bouts of depression. Both he and his
friends trace it to the early days of his childhood. Often left alone in a locked hotel room by his mother,
he was afraid of being abandoned; his feeling of being unloved increased when he was left behind in
Alabama by his unhappy, insecure mother, a woman
who committed suicide when Capote was twenty-
nine. Neither time nor money, nor fame, has been
able to erase the depression which overcomes him
periodically.

Capote believes that his unhappiness comes not
only from what he regarded as desertion by his
mother but also by the betrayals he has felt all his life
by friends and lovers. In recent years he has talked
openly about some of his experiences and has been
frank about his homosexuality. Those sexual adven-
tures started when he was eight (the same age that
he began to write). He had his first romance with an
older boy he met in high school. When that affair
ended, he became the lover of an English professor
from Harvard, a man who left his wife to live with
Capote for several years.

Then, Capote met the man he has described as

the love of his life, the novelist Jack Dunphy. The
two, who have been friends since Capote was twenty-
three, were lovers for fifteen years, most of those years
spent in Europe. Today, Dunphy still resides much of
the time in a house Capote owns in Switzerland. The
two men speak with deep affection of each other,
Capote calling Dunphy his family, the one who would
never abandon him. And Dunphy speaks of their lasting friendship, and the pride they take in their past,
the "terrible past we've held on to and don't talk
about. We . . . stayed young for a very long time." [13]

But there were other lovers as well, sometimes
family men, and, eventually, men of very different
kinds of backgrounds from Capote's. He became the
subject of endless gossip as people saw him take up
with the wives and children of his lovers. There was
also a great deal of talk about his drinking, something
he did more and more to fight depression, but which
was to bring on even greater depression.

While he had been working on *In Cold Blood*, Capote began to take tranquilizers in an attempt to cope
with the pressures of work and the intensity of his
feelings for one of the murderers in the case. In the
years that followed the writing of the book, he kept
increasing the number of pills at the same time that
he was drinking heavily.

He was doing almost no writing. *The Dogs Bark*,
which appeared in 1973, seven years after the publication of *In Cold Blood*, consists of a collection of
essays which had been printed before. Although he
had announced several years earlier that there was a
new book coming out, a novel called *Answered Prayers*, there was no sign of it. Close friends were concerned about his heavy drinking, his drug-taking, his
deep unhappiness. Something had gone wrong, and
he was in serious difficulty with his work and with
his life.

Capote thought the publication of parts of *Answered Prayers* would make everything all right again, a decision that had disastrous consequences for him. The four segments that appeared in *Esquire* in 1975 and 1976 were very different from the stories he had written before. These were stories about the world of the jet set; the characters had real names, or they were obvious to many readers. The substance of the narrative was the gossip he had heard over the years, and many people found his actions unforgivable. Capote's closest women friends dropped him (one of them was as dear to him as Dunphy), and so did many others. The critics disliked the work and said so.

Because of his problems with drugs and liquor, Capote withdrew from the public eye for some time. He published very little following the disastrous response to *Answered Prayers*. But now he is working again, longer and harder than ever before. In the fourth cycle of his life as a writer, the one that began after the publication of *In Cold Blood*, and his last, he claims, he has changed his entire life. He writes constantly and rarely socializes. Also, he has changed his writing style. A story, "Dazzle," recently published, is in the new manner and is autobiographical.[14] There will soon be a new book. Originally, Capote planned to call it *Strange Dents*, but now it is entitled *Music for Chameleons*. *Answered Prayers* may follow shortly after that. Although he is revising the latter, Capote defends it vigorously, and himself as well. The writer, he maintains, must use what he has.

Capote has been compared to Hemingway and Fitzgerald, as having the toughness of one and the charm of the other.[15] The problems of his life and art also suggest theirs in numerous ways—drink, despair, writer's block, sagging careers. Capote is determined to overcome all these, convinced that he must.

For the artist, he says, there is "the integrity of holding on, holding on no matter what." He will not suc-
cumb to the predators, he insists. What matters is to
"just go on doing what you're doing." [16]

2

The Lost Child:

Other Voices, Other Rooms

American literature in the thirties and forties was dominated by social consciousness. The preferred fiction was sociological prose, much of it naturalistic. Thus, when *Other Voices, Other Rooms* was published soon after World War II, it was criticized as being out of the main stream. Within a decade, however, as other young writers gained renown, it became apparent that Capote's novel was a piece of a new pattern in fiction, one that was described by terms such as narcissistic, grotesque, symbolic, and aesthetic.

But some reviewers dismissed Capote's very different type of fiction, for, although they were accustomed to the idea that Southern novelists used gothic elements, Capote's work did not seem familiar. Unlike Faulkner or Tate, he is not concerned with the destruction of a region, the downfall of a class, or the decay of a family. His first novel, as well as those that succeed it, is narrower in scope than theirs. As a result, on occasion his work has been called merely decorative, an example of the overwrought writing of the gothic school. Undeniably, *Other Voices, Other Rooms* belongs to the Southern gothic mode, but it is much more than a baroque fiction. The novelist has combined elements of gothicism with both a Southern setting and Southern characters. The work has mystery and suspense, terror and horror, heavily textured description, strange episodes and people, and psychological and symbolic elements of the gothic. A decaying Southern mansion far removed from ordinary life provides the setting for characters so different from the norm that they are grotesque. But there is purpose in Capote's creation.

The major theme of the novel is homosexuality, a topic considered taboo in American work prior to the advent of contemporary fiction.[1] When the subject did appear in the past, it was usually carefully masked. Capote, however, uses no disguises other than symbols, dreams, and images as he tells the story of a thirteen-year-old boy who becomes an innocent victim of an inescapable fate. In the course of the novel, the boy develops into a tragic figure as he is drawn toward the encapsulated world of the homosexual.

The adolescent boy, who takes a real or metaphoric journey to discovery of self, has been the hero of numerous American novels. Truman Capote's Joel Knox Sansom, of *Other Voices, Other Rooms*, is that kind of traveler. But the Southern gothic world in which Joel becomes entrapped forces him to discover one self, one voice, one room that will imprison him forever. The other Joels that might-have-been are deterministically eliminated as he journeys from the real world of a thirteen-year-old into a surrealistic nightmare from which he can awaken only into another kind of uneality. Joel is an innocent, a victim of people and events over which he has no control.

Other Voices, Other Rooms opens in the middle of a significant journey for Joel, who has come from New Orleans to Paradise Chapel, from which he must travel on to Noon City and finally to Skully's Landing, not surprisingly referred to as "The Skulls" by some of the local people in Noon City. Since most of the trip is described by images of death, the movement from Paradise to Noon to Skulls can also be seen as a

symbolic one from light to darkness, even as Joel's
actual journey takes him from morning to night. Along
the way are "swamplike hollows" that accommodate
strange flowers born in "dark marsh water" containing "luminous green logs" which give the appearance
of "drowned corpses." Darkness, swamps, drowning,
death: these are to become constant images in Joel's
world. A green sky drowns; light drowns; a green
body of water is called Drownin Pond. At times Joel
envisions the house at Skully's Landing as "drowning
in the earth," from which he sees "lilac bleeding out
[of] the sockets of a skull." Images of sweet-scented
lilacs are mixed with memories of April, betrayal, and
a violence that ends in paralysis, a death-in-life. Joel's
world is a chameleon; light, sun, and snow are ambiguous images, suggesting possibilities of freedom,
freshness, and hope but turning later into images of
fear, decay, frigidity, and death. This journey and
several shorter but equally significant ones are set
against an over-lush, over-ripe June landscape which
gives way by the completion of Joel's last journey to
chill autumn, barren earth, and setting sun. The sea-
sonal changes reflect not only the atmosphere in which
Joel lives but also represent changes that take place
in him as one by one the possibilities for normal adolescent life disappear.

Joel voyages to Skully's Landing in the hope of
finding a father he knows nothing of but whom he
imagines to be strong, rich, and heroic. The father
he discovers, ironically, is no Samson, but Ed Sansom,
paralyzed, unable to move, to take care of himself, to
communicate. His mother dead, his father a thing
rather than a person, his only blood relative his Aunt
Ellen back in New Orleans, Joel finds himself in terrifying, nightmarish surroundings inhabited by bizarre
or abnormal human beings.

Some are merely strange in their tastes; some are

freaks; some live on the edge of insanity. But few are ordinary. Between Paradise Chapel and Skully's Landing Joel encounters such people as: a truck-driver who has a toy skull ornamenting his gear shift; a one-armed barber; a female restaurant proprietor with "long ape-like arms . . . covered with dark fuzz," a chin with a wart sprouting "a single antenna-like hair," and a body sagging with "the weight of her enormous breasts"; Idabel, a female-hating girl of Joel's age, regarded as "a freak" by everyone; and Jesus Fever, an ancient retainer of Skully's Landing, described as a "pygmy," a "gnomish little negro," "a sad little broke-back dwarf crippled with age," one who has "yellow, spotted eyes" that suggest magic and things, "a wizard-like quality." Serving as a grotesque Charon, Jesus Fever takes Joel from the comparatively ordinary world of Noon City to the removed, unnatural environment of Skully's Landing.

At the family home in Skully's Landing Joel meets the people with whom he is to live: his paralyzed father, who can communicate only by dropping red tennis balls from his bed; his stepmother Amy, whose ladylike appearance belies an indifferently cruel and deranged personality; Amy's cousin, Randolph Lee, owner of Skully's Landing, an eccentric, amoral man; Little Sunshine, hermit, deviser of magic charms, and resident of the abandoned, decaying, and mysterious Cloud Hotel; and the black housekeeper Zoo, Jesus Fever's granddaughter, who, mutilated and terrified though she is, provides love and limited safety for Joel for a short period of time. Finally, there is one more strange character that Joel encounters when he attempts futilely to run away from Skully's Landing: Miss Wisteria, age uncertain, a dwarf who has a sexual interest in little boys.

Not only do the grotesque characters who enter his life destroy Joel's sense of self and of reality, but also the atmosphere and setting in which he must live erase any link with normal existence. Skully's Landing, with its house, rooms, furnishings, and gardens, is undiluted Southern gothic. The white, pillared house, an old Southern mansion, has an air of decay and death about it. Walls are yellowed or covered with fading paper; candles make flickering shadows against the background, for the house is without electricity. Dark, curving bannisters lead from floor to floor of numerous rooms and hallways. Old mirrors reflect distorted figures. Even the kitchen, dim and abnormally quiet, is suggestive of death: a fly buzzes; "a rusty alarm clock, lying face over on the table, ticktucked, ticktucked." [2] Part of the house lies in ruins caused by a mysterious fire years before. The house, "quiet with emptiness," is "deserted-looking, silent . . . as though . . . captured under a cone of glass." A neglected garden, junglelike in its overgrowth, serves as the landscape. And in the wreckage of the garden on a rotted platform sits a greenly mildewed ancient bell, left from the time of slavery.

The bell becomes an ominous symbol, foreshadowing Joel's fate. On the hot, lonely afternoon of his first day at Skully's Landing, Joel, searching for someone, something, anything, finds the old bell. At the moment of his discovery, Joel glances up to the top floor of the house. There in a window he perceives a "queer lady" unlike anyone he has ever seen before, like a character out of history: a strangely white face smiling; silvery hair set in "a towering . . . pompadour with fat dribbling curls." The vision so stuns Joel that he feels himself and the garden entranced until the curtain falls, leaving the high window empty. With that it is as though a spell has been lifted and Joel stumbles against the bell, which rings out a "raucous, cracked note . . . shattering the hot stillness." The sound of the bell, besides providing gothic atmosphere, also portends a warning signal. Some kind of danger exists for Joel, and that danger is related to the mysterious lady. Joel will hear the bell again, but then it will be tolling in his head, telling him of desertion and absolute loneliness, of the failure of love and hope. He will hear it in the chill autumn of the year, and when "the lady" appears in the window at that time he will accept her and go to her.

That Cousin Randolph is the strange figure in the window is a source of both dramatic irony and suspense for the reader, who sees meaning and intent of which thirteen-year-old Joel on the verge of puberty has no comprehension. The boy notes Randolph's differences from other people, not understanding what they signify. Even when Randolph describes a masquerade ball at which he appeared dressed as an eighteenth-century countess, Joel does not make the connection between that figure and the lady in the window. Joel has little knowledge of sexuality. Although during his boyish wanderings in New Orleans he "had witnessed many peculiar spectacles," and he had found "most puzzling of all, two grown men standing in an ugly little room kissing each other," in Joel's mind Randolph's outlandish appearance and odd behavior do not have any relationship to that enigmatic scene.

Randolph, a man in his thirties, has an ageless look that is both boyish and feminine. He has polished, golden curls, a hairless, talcumed, smooth, peachlike complexion, and "wide-set womanly eyes . . . like sky-blue marbles." He dresses in butterfly-sleeved kimonos, perfumes himself with lemon cologne, wears lady's jewelry on his hands, and on his feet sandals that reveal manicured toenails. Although at first Joel finds Randolph's looks somewhat repugnant and his personality inexplicably frightening, he undergoes a gradual metamorphosis. Because of the series of events that wear away his precarious sense of self, Joel begins to see Randolph as representative of happiness, security, and beauty. At the end, Joel even wants to look like Randolph.

The room in which Randolph spends most of his days and nights is a self-contained world, for Randolph is a man isolated from the ordinary, daily affairs of men. His room seems completely separate from the other rooms of the house as well as the outside. In numerous ways Randolph's room suggests an imprisoned existence. It is suggestive of those gothic rooms where time appears to have stopped, of that place of slow decay, inhabited by a person caught by a betrayal that has immobilized him. Randolph's room knows neither daytime nor night, and because the room, like Randolph, is locked into the past, neither does it know changes of seasons. The faded mirrors in the dim candelabraed room reflect a haunted life; things spill out and settle, caught forever in a moment of time; ragged, disintegrating objects spread over great tables. On Randolph's long, black, heavy table there are ancient dolls, maimed, beheaded, but dressed exquisitely. In his room death-in-life awaits death, for Randolph speaks of his room as a "gaudy grave" and of himself as being dead, of having been born dead.

To embrace Randolph is to embrace death. Unconsciously Joel knows this and struggles against it. But the more he seeks to escape the more paths are closed to him. The intensity of his loneliness as well as his desire for love makes him vulnerable. When those he loves fail him or betray him, each successive instance of loss leads inexorably to the one who waits behind the scenes—Randolph.

Randolph, however, is not content merely to wait. He actively, though secretly, manipulates Joel's fate at critical points. Through deceit he succeeds in hav-

ing Joel's aunt send the boy to live at Scully's Landing; in concealing the condition of Joel's father he
makes Joel's stepmother Amy an accomplice. Considering Zoo, the housekeeper, as something less than
human, he speaks derogatorily of her, helping to
erode Joel's faith and trust in Zoo. He holds a similar
view of the girl Idabel, and after she has run away,
leaving Joel behind, Randolph deliberately burns a
postcard from her bearing a return address, thus re-
moving any possibility of further communication between the two young people. Randolph also surreptitiously destroys letters Joel leaves in the postbox,
letters which are a plea for rescue. And when rescue
does come, in the form of Aunt Ellen (though she
never receives Joel's letters), she does not get to see
Joel. Because she is told he has gone away on a long
trip, she returns to New Orleans. Joel, not understanding Randolph's part in the deception, at that
point believes himself completely betrayed and abandoned, adrift in a sea of green (the color of drowning) loneliness. His surrender to Randolph follows immediately upon his trip to the Cloud Hotel, to which
Randolph has taken him, the abode of the hermit
Little Sunshine.

The visit to the Cloud Hotel is Joel's final journey, and it is the only one he takes reluctantly. Each
previous journey has been an attempt to escape, to
free himself from the encircling web. But each attempt has failed, further undermining Joel's belief in
himself and his masculinity.

At thirteen Joel is in an amorphous stage. Having
reached the end of childhood he must cross the
threshold into adulthood. But Joel has an uncertain
masculinity, in appearance—"too pretty, too delicate
and fair skinned," with large, soft brown eyes that
have a "girlish tenderness"—and in temperament. Having known only the feminine world of his mother and

his aunt, he views the masculine world as mysterious and magical, equating it with abnormal strength and power. He is possessed of many fears, fear of hidden enemies, fear of humiliation, fear of pain, fear of loss and loneliness. These mitigate his desire to escape the sterile future of Skully's Landing for the reality of an existence which has shown him enemies, humiliation, pain, loss, and loneliness.

For a time Joel fastens his hopes of escape on the housemaid Zoo, whom he thinks of as his one friend, his protector against predators. Symbolically, it is Zoo who shoots at the chicken hawks to keep them from killing the chickens. Zoo looks after Joel and shares with him her dream of escape into a new, clean, far-away place, a land of snow. When Zoo leaves Skully's Landing after the death of her grandfather, Jesus Fever, it is with the promise to send for Joel once she has settled into the city of snow. But Zoo never reaches it. Gang raped, tortured [8] along the way, Zoo returns to the Landing bereaved, destroyed, crucified. All hope abandoned, she can no longer believe in snow, in love, in the magical protection of charms; instead she exists in a frenzied religiosity which isolates her from the horrified boy.

Before leaving on her disastrous journey, Zoo gives Joel a very special gift that is intended to protect him against the world, the sword of Jesus Fever. With it, this symbol of masculine strength, Joel feels forceful and unafraid. Yet the power of the sword fails him even as Little Sunshine's magic charms fail Zoo. Carrying the sword with him as he and his friend Idabel unsuccessfully seek out the Cloud Hotel to obtain a magic charm to help them in running away, he attempts to convince himself he is the stronger and braver of the two. When, in order to traverse the wide muddy creek, they must cross on a rotting beam under an old, dark mill, Joel leads the way. However, his boldness quickly dissipates as a cottonmouth snake looms before him. In a paralysis of fear Joel fails to act, so that Idabel seizes his sword, the badge of virility, and with it kills the snake, which may itself be seen simultaneously as a sign of maleness and as a metaphor for Joel. As a result of Idabel's action, Joel's trust in the power of the sword is vanquished and he knows instinctively that it will be useless to go further for the magic charm at the Cloud Hotel.

This is not Joel's only defeat by Idabel, a girl who scorns everything that seems feminine, weak, or soft. Hating her own sex, she refuses to be considered a girl. She longs desperately to be male, insisting that she is like a boy because she doesn't act or think like a girl. Idabel wants to be "brothers" with Joel. But Joel yearns for love, for closeness, for oneness. To him that means a sweetheart, holding hands, kissing, and marrying. Idabel cannot fill that role. Disturbed by Joel's desire for a boy-girl relationship she must constantly prove to him that she is more manly than he is. Because tenderness means femininity to Idabel she hits out at Joel when he attempts to be anything but a buddy. In a telling scene in which Idabel and Joel lie naked in the sun, drying themselves after swimming, Joel, filled with affection for Idabel, kisses her, only to have her turn on him in rage. As they wrestle, Joel falls back, crushing Idabel's rosy-colored sunglasses beneath him. Buttocks bleeding, Joel lies there pinned to the ground by Idabel who is above him. Symbolically the male-female roles are reversed. As Idabel becomes representative of the fierce strength of the conquering male astride the subdued figure of the female, Joel pleads with her to "Stop . . . please stop, I'm bleeding." When she finally releases him she tells him, "You'll be all right."

Joel, however, is not all right. Failure follows upon failure in every relationship, but the humiliations suffered in his encounters with Idabel are the most destructive. He fears her and despises himself more each time Idabel proves herself the stronger of the two. Yet his fear and anger are mixed with love and a sense of loss when he realizes that Idabel has fallen in love with Miss Wisteria, the golden-curled, kewpie-doll dwarf in the traveling show. Although Miss Wisteria makes sexual advances to Joel, he cannot respond. He still has hopes of running away with Idabel, of escaping Skully's Landing. The dream is futile. Separated from Joel at the fair, Idabel goes off with Miss Wisteria, but Joel does not. He returns to Skully's Landing ill and forsaken. Idabel becomes to him "one with the others covered over when the house sank, those whose names concerned the old Joel, whose names now in gnarled October freckling leaves spelled on the wind."

Like the luminous butterfly placed by Randolph inside the lid of the silver compact, like the bluejay killed by Amy for the feathers Randolph collects, like the Creole boy of Joel's age immersed forever in Drowin Pond, like the hanged mule at the Cloud Hotel that becomes the figure in the fire, Joel too will be caught and preserved. He will never become a man, but will remain a boy whose fate is that of the boy in a favorite fairy tale, Little Kay in the "Snow Queen," whose heart was changed by the evil queen into a lump of bitter ice. Though Joel is only thirteen he knows that he is "nearer a knowledge of death than in any year to come: a flower was blooming inside him, and soon when all tight leaves unfurled, when the noon of youth burned whitest, he would turn and look, as others had, for the opening of another door."

When Randolph conducts Joel at last to the Cloud Hotel it is like a rite of passage, farewell to summer and boyhood, passage of autumn and death. The trip through the changing woods and later the strange night spent at the Cloud Hotel are parts of the ceremony Joel must experience before he meets his fate. Whippoorwills lament as sycamore leaves fall in "a rain of October." Beetles, symbols of death, perch "on dying towers of jack-in-the-pulpit." "Gusts of autumn" blow through weeds where not long before there were flowers. The atmosphere sighs of death: "Was, said the weeds, Gone, said the sky, Dead, said the woods."

The Cloud Hotel,[4] a large ruin with a history of tragedy, also suggests little but death and decay, a reminder of Randolph's room: a stopped clock, a fallen chandelier lying in dust, torn draperies resting on the floor, the scuttling feet of rats. It is to this place of death that Randolph brings Joel—Randolph, who has not been there since he was a boy of Joel's age, a child, a sweet boy like Joel, according to Little Sunshine. At the Cloud Hotel the mule John Brown meets its death. When this deathlike journey ends, the boy Joel will turn to Randolph—for there will be no one else—and he will enter the other room. As Randolph and Joel leave the hotel behind, the "morning" resembles an empty "slate." On the tabula rasa, Joel's destiny will be written.

All things have prepared him: loss, fear, loneliness, disaster, deception, desertion. Randolph's encircling web cannot be escaped unless Joel wills it, and he does not. In the late afternoon the two return from the Cloud Hotel. Randolph goes into the house, leaving Joel standing in the garden, where he learns from Zoo that his Aunt Ellen has come and gone. He feels betrayed and when he tries to talk to Zoo, she also leaves him. Overwhelmed by the most intense loneliness he has ever known, even more than that of his first afternoon at Skully's Landing, he hears a bell toll in his head. The summer and boyhood that are ending become the "was," "gone," and "dead" of the au-

tumn woods. Words of finality are brought together
with images of the coming winter, sterility, frigidity,
and death. Clouds darken in the sky and shadows fall
on the garden as Joel looks up to Randolph's window.
There "the lady" waits:

the blinding sunset drained from the glass, darkened, and it
was as if snow were falling there. . . . a face trembled . . .
smiled. She beckoned to him . . . and he knew he must
go: unafraid, not hesitating, he paused only at the garden's edge where, as though he'd forgotten something, he
stopped and looked back at the bloomless, descending
blue, at the boy he had left behind.

3

The Unexplored Realm:
A Tree of Night
and Other Stories

The reception of *A Tree of Night and Other Stories,*
Capote's first collection of short fiction, published a
year after *Other Voices, Other Rooms,* was similar to
the one given his novel: the stories were both praised
and damned for a variety of reasons. The same story
that one critic considered among the author's best was
labeled "derivative and pretentious" by another.[1]
However, while literati still carry on the debate, the
public continues to read the stories and view those
produced for television or the movies.

Because of the distinctly different types of fiction
Capote wrote in the first decade of his career, for the
purpose of discussion critics divided his work into two
large categories: the sunny or daylight stories, and the
dark or nocturnal ones. The sunlight stories are often
comic, somewhat realistic, and sometimes sentimental.
The nighttime stories are concerned with a world of
dreams and nightmares, gothics and grotesques, aber-
ration and evil. The daylight stories are generally told
as first-person narrative and move from the narrator
to the outer world, whereas the dark stories have a
third-person narrator and move to the inner world of
the characters. Not only the short fiction but also the
lengthier works follow this pattern.[2]

The dark stories, written over a period of five
years, are not placed according to date in the original

collection. If they had been, they would appear as "A Tree of Night," "Miriam," "The Headless Hawk," "Shut a Final Door," and "Master Misery." Instead, "Master Misery" is the lead story, followed by "Shut a Final Door," "Miriam," and "The Headless Hawk," with "A Tree of Night" last. Perhaps the author grouped the stories in that order for psychological impact. Although each is about fear and emotional disorientation, it is in the first story and the last that he discusses the source of such upheaval, our childhood terrors and experiences. Whatever his reasons for the first arrangement, in *Selected Writings,* published in 1963, Capote returned to a chronological organization.

Also ignoring the original dates with the daylight stories, Capote interspersed those with the dark stories, but in this grouping there is no obvious plan; the three stories are of descending interest for readers. The best of them, "Children of Their Birthdays" is placed after "Master Misery"; "Jug of Silver" appears after "Shut a Final Door"; and last of that category is "My Side of the Matter," written, Capote has said, when he was seventeen. The weakest story in the collection, it follows "The Headless Hawk," the most complex story in the book and one of Capote's best works. "My Side of the Matter" and "Jug of Silver" were dropped when *Selected Writings* was published, but all the other stories were reprinted.

"Master Misery" is the story of a young girl named Sylvia, who has come to New York expecting to find a more exciting life than the one she has left behind in a small town in the Midwest. The city, however, differs from what Sylvia has imagined, and she finds herself lonely, isolated, and unhappy. Too poor to have a place of her own, she boards with an insipid, insensitive couple, Estelle and Henry, who duplicate the kind of people she'd hoped to leave behind. She despises her job as a typist in an underwear factory; and there is no consolation in friendship or romance, because she is friendless.

To Sylvia the city is cold and indifferent, a place one would go "to get over being in love." Although she tells Estelle she has lost hope of finding someone to care for, and protests when Estelle speaks of the pleasure of lying in bed with a man, many of Sylvia's dreams reflect her desire for love.

Dreams for Sylvia are more exciting than her dreary existence. Thus, one day when she is eating lunch in a cafeteria and overhears a conversation about a man who buys dreams, she decides to seek him out.

That decision ultimately leads to Sylvia's psychic collapse, because Mr. Revercomb, the Master Misery of the title, completes the process of destroying Sylvia's identity. He does what Sylvia is warned against by a fellow victim, taking everything she has, leaving her nothing, "not even a dream."

The descriptions of Mr. Revercomb's house and those of the exterior landscape fall into a pattern the first time Sylvia seeks out the purchaser of dreams. Eventually the inner and outer images become the mirror of Sylvia's depleted life. When Sylvia enters Mr. Revercomb's house, her heels make sounds suggesting ice cubes as she crosses a marble floor, passing an urn of frozen autumn flowers. Although she is indoors, she shivers with cold. And the face of the secretary, Miss Mozart, appears cold to Sylvia, "like . . . snowy . . . wastes." The woman is dressed all in white, wearing a uniform that makes a dry, rustling sound. At another time she is perceived as possessing "green-pale hands." The images, connoting a death-like barren world, are extended when Sylvia leaves

Revercomb's house on a November night; walking on lonely streets as the "dusk" falls "like blue flakes," Sylvia seems totally detached from other people.

Impulsively, she decides to walk through the park, which looks lovely in the evening lamplight. However, her pleasure soon turns to fear as two boys come out of the darkness and begin to stalk her in a suggestive manner. Moving as quickly as she can until she is out of breath, she thinks of tossing her purse to the ground and running, but just then a man with a dog comes along and Sylvia follows him out of the park.

That night, alone in her bedroom, Sylvia feels unhappy, as though something has been taken from her. However, she consoles herself with the thought that the money she can earn from her dreams will enable her to get an apartment of her own.

When Sylvia returns again to Mr. Revercomb's on an icy December afternoon, it is as though the visit has been determined without her willing it. Passing stores decorated for Christmas, Sylvia has a sensation of great loneliness, hating the idea of the oncoming holidays when she feels unrelated to anyone. She shudders as she looks at a large, mechanized Santa Claus, chuckling and rocking; it is as though there is something evil in the figure. Later, in the dark and silent room at Mr. Revercomb's house, Sylvia listens to the sound of a clock, as the walls are shadowed with the reflection of rain on the windows. Again, the inner and outer settings emphasize Sylvia's separateness from others. Descriptions of rain, snow, or dusk appear throughout the story, always encompassing Sylvia.

Sylvia makes friends with Oreilly, a man who was once a clown, but who now has "niente," for Revercomb has taken everything from him. Oreilly is a drunk who has sold all his dreams for whiskey, because he likes to "travel in the sky" [3] and he can't do it without liquor. Master Misery is a creature to fear, Oreilly tells Sylvia. He also indicates that she must have known of him for a long time. Children learn about that terrifying figure from their mothers. It doesn't matter what he is called. He is a thing of chimneys, graveyards, attics, and hollows in trees, what each person secretly dreads.

Sylvia continues to sell her dreams, which soon become endless. Completely isolated in a furnished room to which she moves, she frequently has "phallic" dreams. Fired from her job, she has to sell some of her clothing as well as her wristwatch in order to survive. Soon she loses track of time and becomes disoriented.

Although Sylvia has not taken Oreilly's advice, she continues to meet him often. One night she asks him why Master Misery wants other people's dreams: "What does it mean?" she cries. Oreilly responds that many different kinds of things trigger dreams, but mainly we dream "because there are furies inside of us" which explode. Dreams reveal hidden truths. Because Master Misery is without a soul, he uses the souls of others. Sylvia, Oreilly says, has been robbed of hers.

Sylvia becomes ill and can no longer tell one day from another. She has only an awareness that snow is everywhere, blanketing the silent streets. After losing consciousness she awakens to find Oreilly in her room. He takes care of her until she recovers. One night when she tells him she would like to have back her dreams, he asks her what she would do if they were returned. Sylvia responds that she would go back home, although that means giving up some dreams. Of course those are different from the substance of her unconscious, although she makes no such distinction.

Oreilly persuades Sylvia to ask Revercomb to sell her back her dreams. Although she makes the attempt

it is too late. Revercomb tells her he cannot give her
dreams back because he has used them up. Subse-
quently, perhaps consequently, Sylvia also loses her
only friend. As Oreilly leaves her for "whiskeyberry
pie" in preference to "loveberry pie" she empties her
purse of the few dollars she has left, so that he can
"travel in the blue."

Sylvia is completely alone in the night. The snow
all around her is "like the white waves of a white sea,"
and she is "carried by winds and tides of the moon."
Without compass or anchor she is adrift on a wide,
wide sea. Two boys who come out of a bar stare at
her, and there is the possibility they may be the same
ones who followed her once in the park. However,
this time as she listens to their footsteps behind her
in the snow, she has no fear. She feels nothing, because she tells herself, "there was nothing left to
steal."

Sylvia's sense of destitution has little to do with
her empty purse. The importance of money to live on
palls in contrast with her psychological state. The
physical no longer matters. Even the possibility of
rape does not seem threatening. Perhaps she has lost
her virginity to Oreilly, but it holds no meaning for
her. She no longer has a sense of self. With all her
dreams taken and used up, she has been left only
a hull, resembling the plastic girl riding a bicycle to
nowhere that she has seen in a store window.

The various characters and associative images of
the story take one back to the terrors of childhood,
fear of being lost, fear of the dark, fear of strangers.
Sylvia resembles a child who has lost her way and
cannot find the road back. Even though she proclaims
that she is not a child any longer, much of her behavior is regressive. Embellishing her childish actions
are memories of incidents from early years, remedies
of her grandmother, things she once loved and which

seem more important than her current life. Because she cannot find a place in the adult world of an indifferent city, she retreats to a country of the past.

Sylvia's actions suggest those of Alice stepping through the looking glass. She becomes a small child in a land of bizarre figures and strange landscapes. Everything is distorted as if she were wandering through the twists and turns of a funhouse at a carnival, where terrifying creatures stand in the dark, where unidentifiable sounds create panic, and there is no exit. Mirrors show different selves, none of them alike. Deformed yet somehow recognizable shapes reflect secret fears. In Sylvia's wonderland only the clown has a friendly face, like a "childhood doll," and he sings happy songs; but the clown is used up, "was" he says, hinting of autumn and death. Try as she may, Sylvia cannot find the pleasant circuslike room of her childhood. Her failure to adjust to the realities of grown-up society, which is harsh and mechanical, and the loss of her childhood world leave her bereft and adrift. She becomes a bleak figure, a person without a center, anonymous and barren.

In the story, "Shut a Final Door," Capote uses the technique that he favors in some later works: the creation of the circular effect. It is particularly noticeable in this story, however, because the meaning is enhanced by the repetition of the imagery of the circle. Caught in the web of self-love and self-destruction, the protagonist of "Shut a Final Door" can never escape from his narcissistic personality.

"Shut a Final Door" begins at the end, moves backwards into a recapitulation of certain critical episodes in the life of a young man, and concludes as it began. Walter Ranney, having fled to a "town of strangers," can go no further. Although he has "traveled to the end," that is, the end of his own personal road, there is to be no escape from the fear that has become

his constant companion. Like the ceiling fan he
watches on a hot August night, in a hotel room in
New Orleans, "there was no beginning . . . and no
end."

All of the situations which have brought him to
this point, Walter has created for himself. Shortly after arriving in New York in search of a job, Walter
becomes involved with a number of people whom he
manipulates in order to advance himself. In a pattern
which goes round and round, Walter meets Irving,
who introduces him to his "more or less . . . girl
friend" Margaret, who introduces him to her boss, Kurt
Kuhnhardt, who hires him and introduces him to a
society heiress, Rosa Cooper, who introduces him to
Anna Stimson, an editor, who becomes "a kind of con-
fessor" for him. But in less than a year Walter's com-
pulsive malice alienates each of them, even Anna,
who warns him that he himself is the destroyer in
each relationship.

Irving, the first person to befriend Walter in New
York, is a pink-cheeked, baby-faced young man who
looks "like a boy playing grown-up." When Walter
meets Margaret, who is considering marrying Irving,
he sets about making her his mistress. Margaret talks
about the purity of Irving's love, but Walter enlight-
ens her about Irving's sweetness, saying that he could
never be a husband because he is really "everyone's
little brother."

Margaret's place in Walter's life is very limited.
For a time they are lovers, and she also subsidizes him
until she can get him a job as her assistant at the
advertising agency for which she works. But Walter
uses her only as a steppingstone to friendship with
the head of the agency. Despising the fact that he
works for Margaret, he plans to replace her once his
position is solidified. When Kuhnhardt shows interest
in him briefly, Walter dumps Margaret, and he feels

only hatred for her once he takes up with the young socialite, Rosa Cooper.

It is Rosa's friend, Anna, to whom he tells all his intimate secrets. Perhaps because Walter is convinced that Anna practices every vice, he feels free to confess to her. Yet Anna warns him that everything is pretense or change, and nothing is as it seems. Gold turns to green, mirrors lie, snow is only soap chips. Feeling unloved, Walter asks Anna if she cares for him, and she tells him not to "be dumb," that they are "not even friends." Nevertheless, Anna tolerates Walter until she can no longer bear his malicious gossip about her; he has told people he finds her despicable, that she is a dangerous liar, a "bitch" who covers up "repressed hostility." Unable to cope with Walter's destructiveness, Anna informs him that she wants nothing to do with him.

At last, Walter fulfills his belief that everything in the end comes "finally to zero." His arrogance leads to a critical miscalculation. Although Walter knows Rosa isn't serious about him, he makes the blunder that blows down his house of cards. He invents an item for Walter Winchell's gossip column, hinting of an impending marriage between himself and Rosa. Rosa ends the relationship, and his employer, Kuhnhardt, who is Rosa's friend, dismisses him from his position.

Upon leaving his job, with his aspirations gone, Walter has a surprising sense of relief. Failure has given him freedom, and even peace, because "failure was definite." Walter has always been troubled by indistinct relationships; they reflect his own "ambiguous" feelings. Therefore, even failure is better than not knowing. It brings certainty. After this unexpected revelation, Walter decides that he will leave New York. Suddenly he feels as though a movie is playing inside his head, and he is five years old, at the races with his father in Saratoga. He drinks and

dances around the apartment, returning to a favorite
fantasy that he might have been a professional
dancer.[4]

As the music stops, the telephone rings. It seems
to be only an ordinary ringing of the phone, yet Walter is afraid to answer. The room appears to change
as he stands there. After moments of hesitation, he
picks up the phone, and a "dry and sexless" voice,
"unlike any he'd ever heard before," says hello to him.
When Walter wants to know who it is, he is told that
he knows the caller, that he has known him for a
long time. The conversation ends with "a click, and
nothing." Although Walter soon begins to travel, there
is to be no escape from that voice, no matter where
he goes.

Telling nobody of his plans, Walter takes a train
to Saratoga, where he is a stranger. However, he has
made no reservations, and no rooms are to be had.
A crippled woman he has met on the train takes pity
on him and invites him to her room. In the bedroom,
smelling her strong perfume and looking at her cheap
kimono and the huge black shoe on her clubfoot,
Walter knows he cannot go to bed with the woman.
As he attempts to tell her that, the phone rings.

On the other end of the phone is the same voice
he has heard before, speaking the now familiar words.
As the caller hangs up, Walter begins to weep. He
asks the woman to hold him, and she responds sympathetically. He is a lonely "poor little boy," she tells
him, and like a child Walter goes to sleep in her arms.

But after this incident his nights are sleepless,
as he flees from place to place, until at last he reaches
New Orleans. He can go no further.

Although there are noises of many kinds in the
hotel, Walter feels shut off. In the silent room the fan
goes around and around, like wheels on a train,
like the sounds of voices. His feet seem to him to

resemble stone; his toenails are like mirrors carrying a green reflection.[5] He is afraid of everything, afraid of the heat, afraid of leaving the hotel, afraid of getting lost, for "if he got lost . . . he would be lost altogether." Walter thinks of it as a physical loss, but it is different; this is beyond his will. The familiar identity is slipping away.

This time when the phone rings he cannot answer it. He thinks "an army" soon will come to the door. Like a terrified child he tries to hide in the pillow on the bed, covering his ears to blot out the sound of the ever ringing phone. He tells himself he must empty his mind, "think of nothing things, think of wind." The final segment of the story combined with the title suggests a series of womb images. As Walter's doppelgänger gains strength, Walter's fear forces him to revert stage by stage back to the world of "nothing things," the silent dark room of nonbeing. He cannot confront what the voice on the telephone assures him he knows.

What there is about his other self that causes Walter's disintegration is not as obvious as the story might suggest, although guilt is a major factor in it. But what brings about the guilt? There are clues in the story that tell us it results from something more complicated than Walter's boorish behavior to people who befriended him in New York. Walter is a man who does not seem to know who he is. He has "indecisive" feelings. "He was never certain whether he liked X or not. He needed X's love, but was incapable of loving. He could never be sincere with X, never tell him more than fifty percent of the truth."

Walter's insincerity usually turns to cruelty in relationships, particularly if there is a sexual element. He betrays Irving, who is obviously homosexual. At the end of the affair with Margaret he steals from her. Further, as he looks at the green radio which they

always played when they made love, he decides he
hates Margaret.[6] At Rosa's house he dislikes the
"hearty" college men who are always around, for they
make "green birds fly in his stomach." On one occasion he enjoys humiliating a "nice" and "intelligent"
homosexual he meets, leading him on and then mocking him.

When Rosa breaks off with Walter he has a sensation of bleeding. As he watches a pigeon outside
his window, he picks up a paperweight and throws it
at the bird in an attempt to kill it. He fails and the
paperweight falls to the faraway street. One is reminded of the images of birds in *Other Voices, Other
Rooms* and their connection with the homosexual
Randolph, even though it is Amy who kills the birds
for him.

All of this suggests there is something in Walter
with which he has not come to terms.

One night Anna tells him he is "an adolescent female . . . a man in only one respect." There is also
the matter of his being favored briefly by Kurt Kuhnhardt, "a curious man with a curious reputation."
Kuhnhardt is a bachelor, a man who always has a
protégé, and although Walter knows the arrangement
holds danger and uncertainty he is thrilled to be selected.[7] Walter's secret fears are suggested when he
sees a picture of himself marked red with lipstick and
he has a "sensation of falling in a dream."

But the dream that Walter has on the train ride
to Saratoga is by far the most revealing picture of his
psychological state. In his dream he stands naked on
an empty street as a procession of black hearselike
cars pass him. He doesn't like the feeling that he is
being watched in his nakedness and he calls to the
first automobile to stop. As the car comes to a halt,
the door opens and he sees his father, but when he
goes to the car, his father slams the door, cutting off

his fingers. His father laughs and throws a wreath of thorny roses at him. With each of the cars that follow, peopled by those he has known, most of the same actions are repeated: "Each door opened, each closed, all laughed, all threw roses." He is left there all alone in silence as the cars move on. Screaming, he throws himself on the roses. The thorns open wounds that bleed until rain comes, destroying the flowers and washing the blood from the leaves.

Walter's dream tells of hatred and rejection. Unprotected and alone, he is symbolically castrated by his father, who is the first to victimize him. Following his father's lead, other people in Walter's life repeat his actions: Margaret, who scrawled lipstick on his photograph; Rosa, who rejected him; Anna, who called him a female; Miss Casey, his algebra teacher, who failed him; and finally, Mr. Kuhnhardt, who has with him a "new protégé," a creature without a face.

When Walter's dreams and actions are viewed in combination with the pattern of images that Capote uses, the voice on the telephone begins to acquire form. It is that other self who will no longer be hidden. It is the self that Walter dreads, but one he has known unconsciously for a very long time.

The theme of the double or alter ego appears again in "Miriam." Mrs. Miller, a widow in her sixties, leads a quiet, comfortable existence, but her life is solitary, for she has no friends and only limited interests. A canary is her sole companion. Although she has lived in her apartment house for some time, people seem to be unaware of her. Everything about Mrs. Miller is inconspicuous, her clothes, her hair, her plain face.

Rarely does Mrs. Miller do anything spontaneously. But one night she decides to go to the movies even though it is snowing. As she waits on a long line at the theater, she sees a thin, delicate little girl,

with waist-length, strange-looking hair of silver-white
and enormous eyes that are without any "childlike
quality." Mrs. Miller becomes "oddly excited" when
the child approaches to ask for help in purchasing a
ticket. She learns that the child's name is the same
as her own, Miriam, that she has no last name, that
she has never been to the movies before, and that she
has a very grown-up way of speaking. There is also
something even more unusual about the situation:
when Mrs. Miller asks the little girl's name, it seems
as though she is expected to know it.

A week of heavy snow follows the encounter, a
snowfall that blots out distinctions of earth and sky.
The change of weather distorts the landscape so that
the whole city appears to be deadened, chilled,
hushed, and dark. Even in the daytime there is little
light. Mrs. Miller loses track of time, and when she
goes to a store on Sunday, she finds everything closed.
Her usual isolation has been carried to its most extreme point as though she is the only one on the
silent, empty streets.

That night as Mrs. Miller lies in bed, Miriam
comes to her door. Although it is very late, Mrs. Miller lets her in. Puzzled, Mrs. Miller cannot understand how Miriam located her, since there is no listing
in the phone book. Miriam immediately makes herself
comfortable, praises the apartment but scorns some
paper roses because they are imitation. When she
wants to hear the canary sing, Mrs. Miller won't permit Miriam to wake him, but agrees to prepare something to eat if the child will leave afterwards.

As Mrs. Miller stands in the kitchen she is extremely agitated. She doesn't understand why Miriam
has come. Suddenly, even though it is midnight, she
hears the canary singing, something that has never
happened before. It is even more disturbing when
Mrs. Miller returns to the living room to discover

that the bird's night cover is still on the cage and Miriam is in her bedroom.

In spite of Mrs. Miller's protestations, the little girl removes a cameo from a jewelry box. Mrs. Miller, almost in a condition of collapse, is unable to stand without support, her head heavy, her heart pounding. At that moment she realizes there is nobody she can ask for help: "She was alone; a fact that had not been among her thoughts for a long time. Its sheer emphasis was stunning." Her appearance reflects the emotional shock, as her usually tidy hair falls over her face, which has "mottled" red marks on it. Her eyes seem unfocused. She is completely disoriented. When she refuses to kiss Miriam good night, the child smashes the vase containing the paper flowers and leaves the apartment.

Feeling ill and upset, Mrs. Miller has a number of strange dreams, in which one motif recurs. She keeps seeing a little girl dressed in a white bridal gown, leading a silent "gray procession down a mountain path." Although the destination is unknown, the people follow the child, who looks "like a frost flower." The connection of the dream to Miriam is clear to the reader if not to Mrs. Miller, to whom it is an "elusively mysterious theme." The silver-haired child who visited her was dressed in white silk in spite of the cold weather. Furthermore, the girl whose appearance resembles that of a white flower has destroyed the imitation roses in Mrs. Miller's living room.

When the weather seems to improve one morning, Mrs. Miller decides to go out. The day seems wonderful when she talks with a waitress in a restaurant. But later, after deciding to shop, she strolls aimlessly, uncertain what to do or what to buy. As she walks she looks intently at the people who pass. Everyone seems to be in a hurry, caught up in his own affairs. She has "a disturbing sense of separateness."

When an old man follows her she is afraid, for he looks as if he is mocking her with his grin. Turning onto a deserted street she walks quickly, always hearing the sound of his footsteps behind her in the snow. She comes to a florist shop and enters it, and the old man walks on, tipping his hat as he passes. There is something very strange about him: he smiles but is not friendly. He seems to know something about Mrs. Miller, and the reader wonders whether he is one of the gray procession of Mrs. Miller's dream.

From the florist, Mrs. Miller buys six roses and after that makes "a series of unaccountable purchases . . . as if by prearranged plan." She buys a vase, candy, and pastries; it is as though she is expecting company. There is something strangely disconnected in her actions, for consciously she is frightened of the experiences she has been having, yet paradoxically she is preparing for more.

As Mrs. Miller completes her shopping, the weather changes again. The sky darkens with winter clouds that are "like blurred lenses." The snow begins to fall heavily, so that it covers everything it touches. Mrs. Miller's footprints are obliterated by the time she goes into her house. That evening everything is in readiness when the doorbell rings, but at first Mrs. Miller does not want to let Miriam into the apartment. However, when she does, Miriam announces that she has come to live with Mrs. Miller. The child tells her she has left the old man she lived with. Perhaps, the reader speculates, it is the old man who grinned knowingly at Mrs. Miller on the street, as he followed her in the snow. Upon hearing Miriam's statement Mrs. Miller bursts into tears and fearfully runs downstairs to an apartment on the floor below, in search of help.

After she tells her story to the couple who live

there, the man goes to her apartment to check. But he sees nobody there.

Returning to her own place, Mrs. Miller also finds it empty, "lifeless and petrified as a funeral parlor." She has a sense of emptiness herself, more terrible, she feels, than if Miriam were still in the room. As she looks around in confusion she has to reassure herself of the reality of the river outside the window, of the snow which continues to fall. The room becomes very dark and shapeless. As she rests in a chair Mrs. Miller tells herself that she is all right: "For the only thing she had lost to Miriam was her identity." Soon she feels comforted that she has found a stable Mrs. Miller again, the self-sufficient person "she could trust and believe in," and the thought satisfies her. She has a sense of emerging from a deep, green sea.

Within moments, however, she hears sounds, harsh sounds at first, as though a drawer is being opened and closed again and again. The rustle of silk follows upon that, and it grows in intensity until the entire room becomes "a wave of whispers." Miriam has returned, this time to stay.

Mrs. Miller has lost her hold on reality and has entered the secret, private world of the schizophrenic. She is entrapped forever with the other Miriam, her alter ego, who is everything that she is not—self-assured, demanding, forceful, beautiful, and young. Although Mrs. Miller has struggled to repress that side of Miriam—her secret self—her solitary, loveless, routinized existence has made her vulnerable to disintegration. When the cold winter and snow keep her from her limited contact with others, she can no longer contain the subconscious force that has begun to overtake her. At last the hallucinatory world becomes stronger than the real one.

Capote has said that he wrote the story during

a weekend of heavy snow. Looking out onto a park he thought of a woman haunted by a child who exists only in her imagination. The girl, says Capote, is the woman's "suppressed alter ego. It's herself as a child." [8]

The desire or compulsion to return to childhood is central in the three pieces in which the protagonists are women: "Master Misery," "Miriam," and "A Tree of Night." In each, the female character finds adult life lonely and empty and has a need to escape. There is also a similarity in the images of the three stories, in the constant references to coldness, whiteness, and snow. The background changes in the stories which have males as major figures, "Shut a Final Door" and "The Headless Hawk." In contrast to the frigid atmosphere of the other stories, heat and summer provide a kind of hell in which the deterioration of the characters takes place. And generally, in the two stories about the men, the images are more complex, creating a denser texture to the work than in the parts concerned with women.

The design of "The Headless Hawk" resembles that of "Shut a Final Door" in its circularity. Vincent, the major character, is first seen at the point of disintegration, where he is "never quite in contact, never sure whether a step would take him backward or forward, up or down." The narrative then moves to the beginning, the period when Vincent meets D. J., who is to become his nemesis, traces their relationship, and concludes with the view of Vincent as dysfunctional, unable any longer to act or to resume his normal life.

The chronological details of the story tell of Vincent's meeting D. J. when she comes to the gallery he runs. She wants to sell him a painting she has done, a strange self-portrait of her body and severed head set against the background of a "headless, scarlet-breasted, copper-clawed" hawk. The girl's appearance also is unusual. She dresses "like a freak," has an "indecent" haircut and "depthless eyes" that roll "like loose marbles." D. J. is remote and defensive. She denies even the obvious, her Southern background, as though she does not want to reveal anything about herself.

Yet Vincent is "excited" with a "curious admiration" for her, as well as the painting. The work has a primitive power that draws him. With a sense of recognition, he sees in it "a secret concerning himself," and he decides to buy the painting. The girl also attracts him by her oddity, reminding him of childish feelings he had for "carnival freaks." He knows that he has always loved people who had "a little something wrong, broken." Nevertheless, he recognizes that at the end of each relationship he destroys that same peculiarity which quickened his interest initially.

When Vincent asks D. J. to leave her name and address so that he can mail her a check, she appears confused and fearful. Silently she writes something, then leaves abruptly. Because the information is incomplete, there is no way Vincent can trace her. Nobody seems to know the girl.

Months pass; winter becomes spring. Twice during that time Vincent fancies that he sees D. J., but she always disappears before he can catch up with her. At home Vincent sits in front of the painting, thinking of his directionless life, "a poet who had never written a poem, a painter who had never painted, a lover who had never loved (absolutely)." He begins to regard the hawk as a reflection of the real Vincent, a headless creature. Nothing has ended well in spite of hopeful starts. He sees himself destined to be "a victim, born to be murdered, either by himself or another."

Vincent becomes increasingly tense and irritable. His dissatisfaction with his life brings about an urgent

need to locate D. J., to try to discover how she could
create a painting which captures so perceptively his
own unfulfilled life. Perhaps if he can find her he will
gain understanding. But he fails to recognize the
parallel of D. J.'s twisted decisions to his own or to
apprehend that she is incapable of helping him. He
thinks that an artist who has produced a powerful
work must have great understanding, something he
wants and needs. However, he will learn that the
painting was D. J.'s final creative act before her re-
treat into a fantasy world where she can be a passive
spectator and not a participant.

One April evening at a penny arcade Vincent
sees D. J., who shows no recognition of him. She is like
a sleepwalker, unaware of her surroundings; but when
he asks her to go home with him, she acquiesces
easily. Vincent is pleased with himself and has a re-
newed sense of masculinity, even though D. J. is ap-
athetic, neither responding to nor rejecting the sexual
relationship.

D. J.'s mind is "like a mirror reflecting blue space
in a barren room." She has no sense of time or place.
Moments, days, weeks, months are the same for her.
She rarely speaks, but when she does her conversations center on a mysterious figure whom she calls
"Mr. Destronelli." She insists that everyone is familiar
with Destronelli, the man "who looks like you, like
me, like most anybody." When Vincent insists he does
not know him, D. J. cannot understand why she is
with Vincent. His answer to that is that he loves her,
but D. J.'s only response is to ask what became of the
others he told the same thing.

Vincent doesn't tell D. J. the truth, that he has
betrayed all those who cared for him: his feeble-
minded cousin, Lucile; Connie, a deaf girl; his lover,
Allen, with whom he lived in Havana; and Gordon,

and Helen, and Louise, and Laura. Vincent has been the destroyer—the Mr. Destronelli—for each of them.

The life D. J. and Vincent lead is solitary. Vincent's needs, apart from the sexual, go unfulfilled, and the restoration into wholeness through someone who understands his hidden self does not take place. Although D. J.'s madness is obvious, Vincent does not admit it to himself for some time. Instead of trying to fit her into his normal activities, he follows her into the remote existence of the psychotic. Because of her childlike behavior and strange appearance, Vincent feels he cannot introduce her to anyone, and D. J.'s only interest is in the movies, to which she goes constantly.

The turning point in the relationship comes on D. J.'s birthday. The end is foreshadowed as D. J., pinning to her pillow on the bed the violets Vincent has given her, speaks about the death of flowers.

That night Vincent has a terrifying dream. He is at a party, in a hall that has no exit, "a tunnel without an end." He comments cruelly about the scent of violets to a girl he is dancing with, someone from his past whom he betrayed. He dances with or meets one after another of his victims. And his last partner is D. J.

Vincent finds dancing somewhat difficult because he carries on his back an old man, horrible and ugly, another self. Many of the guests are equally encumbered with "outward manifestations of inner decay." On D. J.'s back there is a beautiful, innocent child cuddling a kitten. It is a reminder of the painting of the headless hawk in which a kitten plays with the hair on D. J.'s severed head. When the child in the dream announces she is heavier than she looks, the old Vincent responds that he is the heaviest of all. D. J.'s burden is her illness, the psychosis which keeps her forever in a child's world of fantasy; but the heavier weight, which is Vincent's, is the burden of guilt, a Dorian Gray corruption that becomes actualized in his nightmare.

Briefly, it seems that Vincent may be freed from his burden. As his hands and D. J.'s touch, the terrible figure floats upwards. However, at that moment the host of the party releases from his wrist the headless hawk that he has been carrying. The hawk circles and dives, and as the claws come towards him, Vincent "knows there is to be no freedom."

Vincent awakens from his dream to find D. J. in the garden. When she whispers that Mr. Destronelli is there, Vincent feels violent. He wants to hit her and he blurts out, almost against his will, "Are you— 'crazy'?" Having spoken the words at last, he is "cold with the death of love." The moon is setting, another symbol of the end of love. And he asks himself why in each person he has cared for he finds always "the broken image of himself."

D. J. has not healed him. Rather, he has become Mr. Destronelli for her, and she becomes an albatross for him. Although he steals home in the middle of the day to lock her out of the apartment, he is never to be free of her. Feverish and ill, he packs her few belongings. He is in a state of collapse as he watches a butterfly [9] flutter in through the window, and cannot bear the sight of it as it settles on the girl's severed head in the painting. The yellow butterfly signifies a mystery to Vincent. Its flight and movement dazzle him. He feels that he must destroy it, slash its wings, as if to violate nature itself. But the butterfly escapes the scissors. Instead they slash through the painting, stabbing the heart of the hawk. Vincent weeps as he cuts up the painting. Looking through tears, he sees reflections of butterflies all over the ceiling of his room, until at last the room is carried into space by the wind created by their wings. [10]

D. J. once told Vincent that she knew Destronelli would eventually kill her. In Vincent's destruction of the painting, more than the possibility of D. J.'s murder is suggested. For if the hawk is himself, as Vincent has said, he is also a victim, perhaps his last—when the betrayer betrays himself.

Vincent's condition becomes one of "nameless disorder" after a long illness that leaves him weak and disoriented. He uses an umbrella like a cane. The very tapping of the cane invokes the idea of a blind man, and there are numerous suggestions of the failure of light. Vincent turns off the light in the gallery as he steps outside to the gray streets. Even though it is summer, the sky is dark. Vincent longs to go away, to find the sun, but he will not be able to do so. He appears to be drifting in a sea, drowning in greenness. Buses become "green-bellied fish"; people turn into "wave-riding masks." [11] The girl on the corner is D. J., dressed in a green raincoat. In the window of an antique store, her reflection is mirrored in green waves. D. J.'s green eyes fasten intensely on Vincent as they stand side by side. When she buys something to eat, it is put into "a green sack matching her raincoat, matching her eyes." Looking at her, Vincent has to convince himself of reality; like a child learning words, he names things as he tries to flee from D. J.

There can be no escape. The two are locked together, going round and round, like the electric fan [12] in the antique store. Wherever Vincent goes, he finds D. J. Once, when he screams out at her, protesting he is not Destronelli, D. J.'s only response is a smile, "because, after all, she knew."

Bound to D. J. always, Vincent is also doomed to be separated from her. The final scene captures the paradox of the relationship. It is evening and storming. Vincent stands in the silence and the rain next to a lamppost when D. J. walks up to him. The sky seems "a thunder-cracked mirror" as the rain falls "between them like a curtain of splintered glass." The revelation of his destructiveness has brought disintegration and psychic death, symbolized by the green waves of the windows, the cracked mirror of the sky, and the splintered glass of the rain.

Vincent, in the end, resembles the other solitaries of the dark stories, whether they are the betrayers or the victims. Without love, they are doomed to turn round and round in a circle that is death-in-life.

The final work in the collection, the title story, tells of a descent into darkness, a fantastic passage into the unknown. All the details of the story build into a crescendo of terror, "the terrors of the shadow of death." [13]

"A Tree of Night" begins with the first unembellished line that sets the mood. "It was winter." The reader, knowing Capote's penchant for suggesting meaning through use of seasons, recognizes that he is entering an unfamiliar landscape, where nothing is as it seems. In the evening world the rain and cold have transformed icicles into "some crystal monster's vicious teeth." Waiting for a train on a cold and windy platform is a young girl named Kay, who is returning to college after attending her uncle's funeral. Except for Kay, the depot is deserted. A figure in grey, she stands there alone. The chill, emptiness, and isolation of the scene are emphasized by the description of the illumination, "a string of naked light bulbs from which all warmth has been drained."

The train, another type of monster, one that spouts steam and glares with light, noisily appears out of the darkness, and Kay enters the hot, decaying interior of the coach. As she makes her way into the car, she is assailed by the odors of "gloomy dead smoke" and rotting garbage. The water cooler doesn't function. The water, usually associated with a life-giving force, here becomes a part of the wasteland image as it runs down to the floor. Kay takes the only seat, located "at the end of the car in an isolated alcove." There her fate will be determined.

"Would you mind if I sat here?" Kay asks the couple sitting on the opposite seat. When the woman's head snaps up as if she has been stabbed with a needle, it is a signal of danger. As Kay settles herself, the train lurches; a ghost of steam hisses against the window and the vehicle moves away from the station. The trip has begun, a journey into nightmare.

The voyage is one for which Kay is unprepared. The clue is given when the woman, hearing that Kay is a college student, states conclusively: "What'll you ever learn in a place like that?"

The woman and her male companion are grotesques. Her appearance is that of a freak, an undersized person with an enormous head and eyes of a sheep. Her dried-out, dyed red hair twisted into large corkscrew curls is covered by a big lavender hat that flops crazily to the side. Smelling of gin, she drinks from a bottle kept inside an oilcloth sack.

Kay becomes fearful of the woman with the sheeplike eyes. The woman's friend also has unusual eyes, "like a pair of milky blue marbles." They suggest cold stone. Because eyes have magical powers in Capote's work, the reader expects the couple to exert a strange influence over Kay.[14] The man, though deaf and dumb, watches her intently and makes peculiar "furry" sounds. Possessing an expressionless face, he looks like an aged child, doused with an odious smelling perfume, and wearing a Mickey Mouse watch. Kay has uncomfortable feelings about him.

As she strums her green guitar, the only inheritance her uncle has left her, she leans her forehead against the window, looking out to the dark Southern countryside; "an icy winter moon" passes overhead. Suddenly the man touches Kay's cheek, bending towards her and staring at her with his "queer eyes." Kay is filled with disgust and loathing, but there is a quality about him that reminds her of something she cannot quite define.

When Kay refuses to drink with the woman, she is intimidated into doing so. There is danger in the woman's smile, a hidden threat. The woman tells her to be a "good girl," and Kay begins to lose her hold on reality. She no longer has control over her own responses. When the woman asks her where she is from, for a moment she cannot remember; it is as though she is lost and has no home. As the conductor passes by, a cold gust blows through the car, increasing the sense of fear, terror of what is to come.

Kay wants to get away from the pair, but the woman will not allow it. She grabs Kay's wrists, telling her, "we wouldn't have you leave us for the world." As "the man's smoke rings mount upward like hollow eyes" expanding into nothing, the reader knows that Kay will not escape the two.

The further separation from reality and descent into darkness is stressed by the passing of another train. Its lights flash on and off as temporarily the lights go out on the coach carrying Kay and her companions. A bell sounds frantically. It can only be a warning. But it comes too late. As the conductor passes again, Kay wants to ask him for help; but she is powerless and incoherent, and he goes away.

Showing Kay a yellowed, ancient handbill, the woman tells the girl that she and her friend earn a living reenacting the story of Lazarus. The man, who plays Lazarus, is buried alive in a coffin. As the woman tells the girl about it, Kay has a shock of recognition; she sees the face of her dead uncle, whom she did not love, as she looks at the man in the opposite seat. The living man has the same terrifying "embalmed, secret stillness" as the dead. Significantly, the woman has described the man's Lazarus costume as a "bridegroom suit." The grotesquerie is intensified when the man caresses and squeezes a shellacked peach seed in an obscene manner, offering it to Kay as a love charm. The woman tells Kay she is rich and can afford the charm. "Where can you get love cheaper, honey?" the woman asks. But the girl, panic-stricken, refuses to pay for the charm. Although she flees to the observation platform, her flight is temporary.

Outside the car, the coldness is penetrating, the sky stark; the train rushes along, and the trees seem pale in the chill moonlight. Shadows are cast by a red kerosene lantern. It is like a landscape of death. Kneeling next to the lantern in an attempt to warm herself, Kay has "a subtle zero sensation" that warns her the man is behind her. She turns to face the man, and looking at him she remembers the childhood terrors that threatened her "like haunted limbs on a tree of night." They were—and are—the fear of "death, omens, spirits, demons," and always "the wizard man."

When the man gestures toward the door, Kay returns to the coach. Everything is completely still. Kay, terrorized, wants to call out, to awaken people. But she is no longer certain anyone will hear her. She wonders if people are really sleeping. Perhaps, the suggestion is there, the people are dead. Thinking she can break the spell, she offers to buy the love charm, "If that's all—just all you want." But of course it is not all. As Kay sinks into a form of unconsciousness, the woman takes her purse and pulls "the raincoat like a shroud above her head."

The shroud is the final emblem of death, completing the series of images Capote uses throughout the story. Many of them recall other Capote works; apart from the obvious, such as paleness, greys, and

blacks, there is the color green, frequently mentioned
in conjunction with visions of death. In *Other Voices,
Other Rooms* it is a drowning color. In "A Tree of
Night" Kay carries death in the form of the green
wooden guitar, itself suggesting the shape of a coffin.
Lilacs, the only flower Kay has ever grown, also appear in *Other Voices, Other Rooms* in connection with
paralysis and manifestations of death.[15] Descriptions
of coldness, snow, and ice fill Capote's pages, as foreshadowing and symbol of entrance into a different
world, sometimes nightmare, often deathlike. Mirrors
and windows change the reality of the landscape like
snow; everything becomes blurred and remote.

In "A Tree of Night" the inner perspective, the
subconscious, blots out the exterior. Kay's fear of
death, which is the loss of self, of identity, becomes
actualized through the figures she meets on her voyage. The embodiment of her terror is the man who
plays Lazarus, the combination of bridegroom and
death: dressed in marriage clothing, carrying a love
charm, deaf and mute, death's representative seeks
out Kay.

A case might be made for some of the resemblances "A Tree of Night" bears to the Persephone
myth, or at least to a part of it: the young virgin
who travels into the realm of Hades. The car, the passage, the scenery, the conductor, the atmosphere become part of a journey into an underworld. But the
second half of the tale remains untold; we remain uncertain whether Kay will ever be able to return to a
world of light and hope and renewal.

Of the daylight stories in the collection, "Children
on Their Birthdays" is the most familiar and one of
the most popular of all Capote's pieces. It was written
the same year that *Other Voices, Other Rooms* was
published, 1948, thus illustrating the divided stream
of Capote's talent. Although the reader can discern

some similarities between the two works, more obvious links are to be found between the short story and *Breakfast at Tiffany's* and *The Grass Harp:* a young man gives an eye-witness account of the events, but almost nothing is known about him in "Children on Their Birthdays," for he does not appear to be a participant in the action as are the young writer in *Breakfast at Tiffany's* and Collin Fenwick in *The Grass Harp.* The plot and setting are realistic and the characters have none of the grotesque qualities we associate with the dark works. "Children on Their Birthdays" has a tender tonal quality that recalls both *Breakfast at Tiffany's* and *The Grass Harp.*

Once again, as in two of the dark stories, the pattern is circular. We are told the ending first; the story then follows and develops chronologically to the conclusion, which reiterates the statement made in the introductory sentence.

The major figure in "Children on Their Birthdays" is a young girl named Lily Jane Bobbit, always referred to as Miss Bobbit. A forerunner of Holly Golightly, the heroine of *Breakfast at Tiffany's,* Miss Bobbit is mysterious, ambitious, very attractive to males, worldly-wise, generous yet self-centered. Furthermore, she is unusually precocious, a ten-year-old who wears cosmetics, walks and talks in a studied manner, and even interjects a word or two of French into the conversation as Holly does. "Merci you kindly," says the figure-conscious, skinny Miss Bobbit in rejecting tutti-frutti ice cream because it is not good for the figure. Miss Bobbit, like Holly, was modeled after an actual person that Capote knew.

Miss Bobbit arrives in town with her mother one hot summer evening on the six o'clock bus from Mobile. It is never known why the Bobbits come, and they intend to be temporary residents, because Miss Bobbit is only waiting for her big chance to go to

Hollywood. When they get off the bus, they stop for directions at Billy Bob's house, where most of the children of the town are celebrating his birthday. Miss Bobbit makes a strong impression on everyone with her looks and mannerisms. Although her mother is with her, it seems as though the child is in charge, for she makes the introductions, asks the questions, and provides whatever information she deems necessary for the group to have, particularly the announcement that her mother earns their living as a seamstress.

In a figurative sense, Miss Bobbit is another orphan figure. Her father, a criminal, is in prison in Tennessee, and she has no contact with him. Her mother, who is either mute (according to Miss Bobbit), or foreign (according to their landlady), never speaks to anyone. Miss Bobbit looks out for herself as if there were no parent. And soon she begins to direct the lives of a number of other people. When she starts a magazine subscription business, she has the local boys delivering purchases for her for a commission. She makes an undying friend of a black girl, Rosalba Cat, when she defends her against the bullying of Billy Bob and Preacher Star; as a result, Rosalba, like Catherine with Dolly in *The Grass Harp*, devotes herself to Miss Bobbit. And Miss Bobbit is the person who sees to it that a swindler, who has duped many people of large amounts of cash, is traced, caught, and forced to return the money.

Although Miss Bobbit violates any number of community practices and a few laws—she won't go to school or church—adults all admire her. So do the boys, who ignore the other girls once Miss Bobbit comes to town and exhaust themselves trying to win her affection.

Miss Bobbit, however, has no interest in romance. The boys may win her approval but not her love. There is a type of sexlessness about Miss Bobbit, in spite of her beauty. Although she dresses in a very feminine way, wearing frilly skirts and blue-lace underwear, and sings suggestive songs, she is all business. When contrasted with her, the boys who are several years older than she is seem to be silly adolescents. Furthermore, Miss Bobbit pays no attention to sexual mores. In a brief scene reminiscent of the swimming episode of Joel and Idabel in *Other Voices, Other Rooms,* Miss Bobbit gives Billy Bob an alcohol rub "from head to toe," when he has an upset stomach. Even though she is reprimanded by the boy's mother, she thinks nothing of it. Miss Bobbit is unconcerned with "whether it's nice or not," and equally indifferent to masculine ardor.

Miss Bobbit's claims to have had a great deal of experience seem valid as she goes about her life. However, her reasoning often runs contrary to that of others. In the matter of religion, she avoids churches because the smells offend her; she volunteers the information that she loves and trusts the Devil to help her get ahead in her career. After all, Jesus doesn't care for dancing.

Her intention is to become famous, and she spends her time readying herself for the moment when her chance will come. She sings and dances and practices comedy routines all in the hope of getting to Hollywood. When she wins the amateur contest put on by Manny Fox, the man who turns out to be a thief, it seems as though she is on her way. Temporarily thwarted when Fox absconds with the money, Miss Bobbit goes to the effort of seeing justice done. After the money is given back, she then persuades the people, who had paid Fox, to invest in her, for surely she will be a great star one day. Her persuasiveness works. She gets the funds to go to Hollywood. Ironically, however, the evening that she is to leave she is killed by the six o'clock bus as she runs out to take the

armloads of roses held by her admiring swains. It has
been a year since the bus brought her to town.

In the year that she lived in the town, says the
narrator, "nothing she ever did was ordinary." There
is a magic and wonder about her that gradually con-
verts people to her way, for "whatever she did she
did it with completeness, and so directly, so solemnly,
that there was nothing to do but accept it."

Like Holly Golightly, Miss Bobbit is a wanderer,
searching for an ideal. She has not yet found where
she belongs. Holly's desire is to discover a world of
beauty and calmness that Tiffany's gives her; Miss
Bobbit dreams of a place "where everything is dancing, like people dancing in the streets, and everything
is pretty, like children on their birthdays." Both girls
speak of living in the sky. However, Holly, older and
more knowledgeable than Miss Bobbit, recognizes that
the sky is an empty place; yet she never succeeds in
finding her Tiffany's. Miss Bobbit believes that living
in the sky can bring one fame and riches. Since she
is only a child when she dies, she does not undergo
the disillusionment that adulthood brings. At her
death, her future remains both untouched and un-
tarnished. To complete the image there is the picture
of her as she readies herself to leave town. Miss Bobbit
is clothed all in white, even to the parasol she carries.
The narrator describes her as looking "as though she
were going to Communion."

The Southern background emphasizes the harmony of the story. Although the period of time during
which all the episodes occur is a year, it seems always
to be summer, but a summer of mulberry trees, yellow
roses, and sweet shrub; blackberries and dust; eve-
nings "blue as milkglass," and night-blooming irises.
Neither autumn nor winter intrudes at any point;
although the word "February" is used when the

amateur program takes place, there is no other reference to that season.

Miss Bobbit dies in summer, running toward "moons of roses." The image fits the brightness of her personality, the white communion look, and the untainted future where everything can be caught forever in beauty. There is neither cold wind blowing nor yellow autumn leaves falling as in the later *Breakfast at Tiffany's;* no fall-reddened Indian grass sings its songs of the dead as in *The Grass Harp;* and no hint of chill sun or snowflakes or "was" or "gone" creates an air of sadness as in *Other Voices, Other Rooms.* Only the rain, a frequent image used by Capote to suggest nostalgia and the passage of time, links the ending of this short story to the three novels. But the rain that comes at the conclusion of "Children on Their Birthdays" is connected to the earlier images of the story as it falls "fine as sea spray and colored by a rainbow."

"Jug of silver" might easily be labeled a Christmas story. It has all the qualities associated with that genre: the holiday season with its trimmings of holly, fruitcake, and trees covered with snowflakes and tinsel; a plotline involving a child's wish and fulfillment of happenings; a reward for the deserving poor; the quality of magic; and finally, an annual retelling of the events that transpired.

The narrator recalls an important event in his boyhood when he worked after school in a drugstore owned by his uncle, Mr. Marshall. When a new and more modern drugstore is opened across the street, Mr. Marshall decides he has to counteract the damaging effect to his business. He fills an empty wine jug with nickels and dimes and invites customers who spend a quarter in his shop to take a chance on guessing the amount of money in the jar. The person who will come closest to the correct figure will win the entire sum on Christmas Eve. The gimmick works and business becomes better than ever.

Among those who come to the store are two poor children, Appleseed and his sister Middy. The boy is desperately anxious to win the money although he does not give his reason until his desire is fulfilled. It is to buy his sister a set of false teeth so that she can be a movie star. Appleseed's guess about the coins is perfect. To the delight of Mr. Marshall, his close friend Hamurabi, and the narrator, the money can go to the one they want, the strange, intense little boy.

Appleseed stands apart from other people in the story. He is a stranger who lives on a farm three miles outside of town and about whom very little is known. He claims to be one age, but his sister says he is another. He is small and frail looking, badly dressed all the time in the same outfit, and "always cold." Appleseed is like the wizard figure familiar in certain other Capote stories, both the dark and the light. The narrator speaks of the boy's "green eyes that had a very wise and knowing look." Like Dolly Talbo (*The Grass Harp*), who also has green eyes, Appleseed is a good kind of wizard figure.

He has only a single name, one that suggests a mythical character out of American folklore. Further, Appleseed is certain that he has magical powers because he was born with a caul. He believes in witchcraft and tells Hamurabi that a witch he knew "put a hex" on his mother. Although Appleseed claims that he is able to count the money in the jar, nobody believes him. He comes to the drugstore day after day, even during the coldest part of the winter, in order to study the jug so that he can get the exact figure. When Appleseed wins, the narrator asks Middy how her brother was able to know the amount. Middy announces that he counted and prayed, and then she refers to the caul with which he was born, the magical or wizard quality he possesses.

Inasmuch as there is no other explanation for the feat, that one must stand. Capote increases the idea of the unknown, the inexplicable, the mysterious, by calling Mr. Marshall's friend Hamurabi, a name that suggests great ancient kings. And the drugstore is called Valhalla. In Teutonic myths, the souls of heroes are received in the hall known as Valhalla. Mr. Marshall's store is a beautiful, elegant old place, with an antique marble soda fountain, and mahogany framed mirrors that reflect faces as if by candlelight. The atmosphere is special, one where magical things can happen. It is fitting that Appleseed's dream of winning happens there.

The other part of his dream does not come true, however. Middy does not become a famous star. But the boy gains a type of fame; although he and his sister move away from the area, they are not forgotten. Appleseed becomes a legend. His is a story Mr. Marshall tells the Bible class every Christmas.

"Jug of Silver" bears some resemblance to "Children on Their Birthdays," although it is a much more sentimental story. In both, the narrator looks back, remembering a very special child, one who was different from others and who left his mark on the town. Each had great dreams, as well as a longing for a better life. Part of the dream was of the fame and fortune that movie stardom would bring. And neither gets his heart's desire.

"My Side of the Matter," though a part of *A Tree of Night and Other Stories,* bears little resemblance to the fiction in it which otherwise fits the two categories generally assigned, daylight and nocturnal. The only similarities are in the setting, a small Alabama town, and the first-person narration by a young man.

Briefly, the narrative concerns the battle between

Sylvester, the narrator, and his wife's unmarried aunts, with whom they have gone to live. The young couple, both sixteen, have been married only three months when Marge, the wife, becomes pregnant and insists on returning home. Because of the move Sylvester is forced to give up what he calls his "perfectly swell position clerking at the Cash'n' Carry," and after that he makes no attempt to find work again.

The aunts, who dislike the narrator at first sight, will not do anything for him. They refuse to lend him the family car, convinced he knows nothing about driving; insist he sleep on the porch although his wife gets back her bedroom; deny him cigarette money; and give him only cold yams and leftover grits for meals. During the short time they all live together, the aunts fight bitterly with Sylvester, insulting him and nagging him, and finally attacking him physically. The story ends as Sylvester barricades himself in the parlor.

Although the aunts as seen through Sylvester's eyes are harridans, Sylvester is by far the worst one in the group. He is vain, selfish, arrogant, and lazy. In addition to stealing, he is not averse to blackmailing people or accepting bribes. And he is a sneak who pries into everybody's affairs quietly and surreptitiously.

The character of Sylvester is revealed much as in the dramatic monologue form. He tells more than he knows, and the reader sees irony of which the narrator is unaware. The irony succeeds, but the humor fails. The plot is too sketchy and the characters too stereotyped to be effective.

Not surprisingly, the story has been ignored by critics and anthologists alike. But it was written by a very young writer, whose work matured rapidly into the powerful and memorable stories that comprise the collection.

Capote as a child with his cousin Miss Sook Faulk, who was the inspiration for the loving, eccentric spinster of numerous Capote works.

Capote at the age of 23, after writing his first novel, Other Voices, Other Rooms. The Bettmann Archive, Inc.

The young Capote. The Bettmann Archive, Inc.

Capote, as host of the celebrated private party held at the Plaza Hotel in New York in 1966, arrives with the guest of honor, Katherine Graham. Mrs. Graham wears the black and white mask which was a must for the 540 guests. Wide World Photos.

Capote stands in the living room of the Kansas ranch house where four members of the Clutter family were murdered in 1959. This event was the basis of his "nonfiction novel," In Cold Blood. Wide World Photos.

Capote (left) with his friend Lee Radziwill and Norman Mailer at a cocktail party given by Ladies' Home Journal *in 1972 to mark publication in that magazine of a "preview" of Lee Radziwill's forthcoming book* Opening Chapters. UPI.

Capote (left) with Andy Warhol at a party in 1979 at Studio 54 celebrating the tenth anniversary of Warhol's magazine Interview. UPI.

Truman Capote played a key role in Neil Simon's film Murder by Death. *From left to right: Capote, Elsa Lancaster, Estelle Winwood, Peter Faulk, David Niven, Maggie Smith, and James Coco*. The Museum of Modern Art/ Film Stills Archive.

4

Paths of Memory:
The Grass Harp

The Grass Harp, which was published two years after *The Tree of Night and Other Stories,* has many bonds to both earlier and later works. Here the magical, fairy-tale atmosphere is sunny, the return to childhood happy. Growing up is pleasurable for the boy in this novel because he has, at least for a few years, the love of an elderly woman relative.

Most of Capote's work, whether labeled "fiction" or "nonfiction" or "nonfiction fiction," contains autobiographical elements. Consequently, it is fitting that this idealized portrait of a childlike older woman is dedicated to Miss Sook Faulk, "In memory of affections deep and true."

The struggle between innocent naturalness and restrictive societal values is basic to the meaning of *The Grass Harp.* Although in the long run the rules of society prevail, it is not as if goodness is defeated by a corrupt force. Rather, it is the recognition that compromise is necessary for the continuity of a community. Thus, over a brief period of time, all the important characters of the novel are touched and changed by the events that occur. Each person gains some self-knowledge as well as understanding of others.

Set in a small Southern town, far removed from the busy mainstream of modern life, the story concerns Collin Fewick, his relatives, and his friends.

Collin, as narrator, tells of his past personal history between the ages of eleven and sixteen, the times he calls "the lovely years." But the tale is not only Collin's; it belongs equally to the elderly but simple-hearted Dolly Talbo. Central to the work are Collin's search for love and identity and Dolly's realization of the complexity of life, a recognition that results in her loss of innocence about human nature.

Because his parents are dead, buried on the edge of town, in the Baptist cemetery "of bonewhite slabs and brown burnt flowers," Collin is raised by Dolly and Verena Talbo, two maiden ladies who are his father's cousins. Collin loves Dolly, the gentle, guile-less sister, but he scorns Verena, who is a successful businesswoman and property owner. The materialistic values of Verena have no more appeal for Collin than she does, for he prefers the simple ways of Dolly and her devoted Negro-Indian friend, Catherine.

In a variety of ways Collin bears a strong resemblance to Joel Knox of *Other Voices, Other Rooms*. Like Joel, Collin is an orphan figure, an adolescent boy who lacks many of the more flamboyant masculine traits. Collin chooses a sendentary, quiet existence over a vigorous athletic one. A shy boy, he doesn't participate in the activities of other children, and he is more comfortable in the company of older females than he is with youngsters of either sex of his own age. He has a delicate appearance, looking smaller than he actually is, though with the help of Dolly's companion, Catherine, he is "stretched" to a normal height, and has the notches on the pantry door to prove it. Sensitive, emotional, and imaginative, Collin is a lonely young man until his cousin Dolly becomes aware of his need for companionship and includes him in her very special world, the one she has shared previously only with Catherine.

Dolly knows all about nature, but nothing of the

world or ordinary matters. Catherine, who grew up in the Talbo household, makes up "facts" as they occur to her, but it doesn't matter very much, since she is comprehensible only to Dolly. It is Verena who has the type of intelligence that the community understands, even though she is feared and disliked by a number of people. Verena is the one that "was always introducing a new rule or enforcing an old one." To Collin she is "like a lone man in a house full of women and children." Verena travels to St. Louis or Chicago on buying trips for her businesses; but Dolly has never been more than sixty miles from home, and that was only once in her life.

However, Dolly has no need to travel. She finds great joy in the natural world around her, and she also has a vocation exclusively her own. As the inventor of a remedy for dropsy, Dolly has developed a following of people from all over the state who buy her special cure and seek her advice about their various ailments. A good deal of Dolly's time is spent writing letters in which she warns customers of various health hazards. For example, she cautions one correspondent: "Do not touch sweet foods," an amusing suggestion, inasmuch as Dolly herself "lived off sweet foods."

The only contact Dolly has with society comes through her mail. For most of her life her only friend is Catherine. Dolly goes nowhere, except to River Woods once a week to collect the herbs, leaves, and roots she needs for the dropsy medicine. She brews the dark brown liquid in a great iron tub, stirring the mixture with a part of an old broomstick, while the fascinated Collin watches, describing himself and Catherine as "apprentices to a witch." Indeed, the manner in which Dolly gained her knowledge of the remedy is like a folktale. In her childhood, she befriended some gypsies, who rewarded her by teaching her a rhyme which listed the ingredients of the medicine and the techniques of making it, "if you want a dropsy cure."

Dolly shares her earnings with Catherine and Collin, spending everything she gets. They buy all the toys, games, and lessons that catch their eyes in magazines, including an item bought to assuage Collin's desire to have a secret language that only the three of them would know. To please him, they buy and briefly study a book of French from which Dolly learns a word or two, and Catherine masters a sentence that she claims will fulfill her total need for another tongue: "Je suis fatigué."

Among the three of them, the funniest is Catherine, whom the world cannot understand and therefore treats as an inferior, regarding her as a black "mammy." She is the most adventuresome and the most cynical. Catherine's feelings are strong. Verena, Catherine has always disliked intensely. "That One" is the name she uses to refer to Verena, a term reflecting her distrust. But Dolly she calls "Dollyheart," no doubt a variation of "sweetheart." Catherine is devoted to Dolly, "and everything they had to say they said to each other." After Dolly's death, Catherine tries to hold on as long as possible to the feeling that Dolly is still with her. She changes her eating habits to resemble those Dolly had; she wears Dolly's clothes until she cannot fit into them. In time she removes from her mouth the cotton wads that made her speech somewhat intelligible, thus cutting off any possibility of communication with other people; and she retreats into a solitary existence. Having cared for Dolly all her life, Catherine has no further interest in anyone, not even Collin, once Dolly is gone. She has "put down the load," says Catherine.

For most of the years that Collin spends in the Talbo home, life follows a regular pattern. Everyone's place and role are set. Verena, the richest person in the town, is the owner of numerous businesses. Stern and sharp, incompatible with other members of the household, Verena leaves them to the running of the house, while she works late at night on financial matters. Verena is the decision maker as well as the money maker, filling a traditionally masculine function in the family. Dolly and Catherine perform the domestic chores: they cook and clean, tend the garden, and care for the chickens.

The rooms of the house reflect the personalities of the owners. Verena's room is furnished like an office, with a business desk, ledger books, and filing cabinets. Dolly, whose name suggests her childlike qualities, has a bedroom symbolic of her innocence and youthfulness. On the one hand, it is a place in which "a nun might have lived," and, on the other, it is a little girl's room, all pink walls, floor, and furniture. So significant is the color pink to the reader's understanding of Dolly as eternally young and virginal, that it is a link to what kind of person she remains until her death. Even in the last few weeks of her life she has the untouched, shining sweetness of a child. When she gets her first radio, Collin paints it pink so that it will be acceptable before putting it in her room. Although the radio suggests a link with a larger world than she has known, Dolly continues to live in a uniquely personal environment. Dolly turns her station to football games in spite of the fact that she has no understanding of the sport. She listens because she likes the shouting sounds that seem to her to be full of happiness. She thinks life is meant to be lovely, like the color pink.

A favored room of Dolly and Collin is the attic, which they reach by climbing a ladder inside the linen closet. There are all sorts of children's treasures in the attic, including boxes of things Dolly has saved since she was a small girl. The attic is a room to play in, to hide in, a place from which one can look down into the rooms below, a child's world in which Dolly and Collin first become friends, and finally the room in which Dolly suffers her fatal stroke as she dances around in her last game with Collin.

There is also another special room, the kitchen, which is shared by Dolly, Catherine, and Collin. All the winter days after school, Collin hurries home to be with Dolly and Catherine in the warm, fragrant kitchen. Most of the pleasures they enjoy exist there: bread and cakes and candies bake in the oven, as the coffee bubbles on the stove, in contrast to the "zero blue breath" of the frost on the windows. A geranium plant blooms constantly, in defiance of the season; goldfish swim in a coral castle, and pictures of kittens cover the walls. There are rocking chairs and a hook rug, a woodstove, and a fireplace. The kitchen is the room where Collin does his homework, where the three of them enjoy all the pleasures of children, and in which they weave their magical tales. It is a sanctuary for Collin. When he remembers it many years later, filled with the sweetness of memory, he asks: "If some wizard would like to make me a present, let him give me a bottle filled with the voices of that kitchen, the ha ha ha and fire whispering, a bottle brimming with its buttery sugary bakery smells." The "lovely years" of his boyhood are recalled in those images, the days that were all too brief.

When Collin is sixteen, things change very suddenly. The upheaval occurs because of Dolly's success with her dropsy remedy. Verena becomes aware of the financial possibilities of producing and marketing the medicine commercially, on a scale very different from that used by Dolly. After Verena discovers that Dolly's simple operation is sufficient to be taxable, she buys an old canning factory, which she has rebuilt, orders expensive machinery for it, and brings in Dr. Morris Ritz from Chicago to run the operation. However, Verena has not considered the idea that Dolly will refuse to go along with her plans. A bitter quarrel ensues when Dolly refuses to give up her secret formula, "the only thing that has ever been mine." Infuriated, Verena tells Dolly she is ashamed of her and Catherine and blames Dolly for the unhappiness of her lonely life. Dolly is deeply pained and she responds that she and Catherine will go away.

Although Verena does not believe what Dolly has said, Dolly carries out her promise. She and Catherine prepare to leave the house. Shortly before morning, while Verena is asleep and everything is quiet, except for the faraway sound of the stirring roosters, Dolly comes to say goodbye to Collin. But he insists on joining her and Catherine in the tree house where they are going to stay until they make their future plans. Dolly agrees, recognizing Collin's fear and distress, his feeling of being abandoned by those he loves. And so the three of them set out for River Woods, where the old tree-house is.

In a lyrical passage filled with symbolic implications, the scene is described. Collin hears the sound of the town clock as he dresses for the trip that September dawn. He has been half dreaming of the autumn winds moving through the sleeping town; as the sun comes up they reach the field of Indian grass, which has turned scarlet with the season. Beyond are the woods and the house in the China tree, which is "a September bowl of green and greenish gold." The striking colors of the season, the gentle breeze, the dew of the morning are all filled with loveliness, but it is fall and a clock has tolled. There will be a "few autumn days" that will serve for "a monument and signpost." Many things will happen within a short time. Much will be learned, and several lives will be altered.

The world that Collin, Dolly, and Catherine enter is an idyllic one. There in the Chinaberry tree no rules exist. Everyone is at ease as the effect of the tree removes old boundaries and creates a climate of friendliness and truth. Dolly, though dressed formally in a woolen suit and veiled hat for traveling, loses her shyness; soon Catherine becomes more outspoken than before; and Collin makes friends with a young man, Riley Henderson, whom he has admired and envied, but who never even noticed him previously.

Riley is the first intruder into the tree world. When he inadvertently lets others know where the trio is, a group of townspeople, including Sheriff Candle, agent of the law, and the Reverend Mr. Buster, representative of religion, arrive in the woods to attempt to persuade Dolly to return to her home. However, one of the townspeople, Judge Cool, immediately joins the rebels and urges them to fight the forces that are imposing societal standards on them. A skirmish follows as Judge Cool attacks the Sheriff. The outsiders are routed, but the Sheriff warns the winners that their victory will be of short duration.

The battle scene provides a vaudevillian touch to the tree-house segment of the story. Although other humorous episodes occur in this section, the tale of the invasion by various members of society is heavier, more contrived, and less comic. People grab one another, slide down trees, and fall or throw themselves on top of others; Dolly pours orangeade inside the Sheriff's shirt, and in her confusion drops the empty mason jar from the tree onto the head of the minister's wife. The comic intent is not realized. Consisting of nonverbal humor which succeeds on stage or on film but does not work without visual aids, the scene fails to be funny.

In contrast to the forced amusement of the invasion episode, there is a delightfully funny, albeit nonessential story of a traveling evangelist and her fifteen children. The star of the brood is named Little Homer Honey, and it is because of his appeal that large collections of money are taken in, for Little Homer Honey is advertised as being able to "Lasso Your Soul For The Lord." Sister Ida and her children travel in an ancient truck from state to state, holding revival meetings as their way of earning a living.

The Southern Bible Belt has long been the favorite area of the country for evangelicals. Various religious groups are indigenous to the region. Collin notes: "Revivalists are popular in this town; it's the music, the chance to sing and congregate in the open air." Because Capote is able to build his humor on the reality of the revivalist movement, it becomes a very attractive form of comedy. He introduces a picaresque element as Sister Ida and her assorted offspring, including the Child Wonder, hold a prayer and entertainment meeting in the town. When the children start taking in contributions of bills hung on "God's Clothesline," the Reverend Mr. Buster confiscates the money and sees to it that the evangelicals are run out of town.

Eventually Sister Ida and her children end up in River Woods, where they meet the tree-house dwellers. Their brief stay provides the opportunity for more humor, including Sister Ida's story of the way she got the spirit of God. After she discovered she had been chosen and knew what her "task was to be," she became something of an Ancient Mariner in carrying the Word from place to place. Along the way she acquired one husband, who disappeared, and her large family, most of them illegitimate. In spite of their difficulties, they are a happy, loving group whom the rebels take to their hearts. Dolly gives the evangelists all the money she and her friends have, as well as the Judge's gold watch, and when Sister Ida and the children prepare to leave they ask Dolly and the Judge to go with them. But of course that cannot be, and the diverting interlude comes to an end.

Humor in *The Grass Harp* has a wide range: there is situational comedy as well as comic characters, verbal humor and physical humor. Some of it consists of slapstick stage business, such as the battle scenes; some depends on regional elements, such as the stories involving Sister Ida; some suggests the influence of burlesque in sexual humor, as in Collin's description of an invitation to visit the town jail to witness the sight of an unusually endowed young man; and some of the comedy depends on the reader's enjoyment of the tall tale. Although Capote frequently enlivens his work with humor, *The Grass Harp* contains more comic components than any of the author's other works.

Between the two humorous scenes of the battle and the revival meeting, action significant to the story has taken place. Catherine is arrested and put into jail when the Sheriff returns with deputies and a warrant. Riley is shot in the shoulder and has to be taken to a doctor for treatment. The violent happenings quickly bring about the resolution of the story.

The group of people who have assembled in the tree house are all independent spirits. In one way or another they have rejected the precepts of the community. Dolly has refused to accept a high evaluation of money as a means of success; Judge Cool does not want to live the regimented existence his sons and their wives have decreed for him; and Riley Henderson is unwilling to curb his independence in order to please others. However, all three find that they cannot really separate their lives from those of their families and neighbors. But they must find a satisfactory way to return to the community.

When they first come together, each of the five

feels like an outcast, a homeless being. The Judge expresses their mood when he says, "It may be that there is no place for any of us." Yet, he notes that their happiness does not depend on finding a permanent home. Perhaps what matters most is a feeling of belonging, even if it is very brief, ephemeral. Although Judge Cool is the advisor, guardian, and father figure, each member of the group has something to give the others. Sharing secrets, banding together, uniting in thought and affection, each develops the will and strength to be both individual and the "leading citizens" that prevent "the entire place from going to pieces." Because of the shared experiences, they are able to return to the community with greater understanding than they had before of themselves and of the people with whom they have spent their lives.

Riley settles down at last, and eventually becomes an outstanding figure in the town. Having learned trust, he falls in love and marries Maude Riordan. Collin discovers much about friendship and love; however, he also learns that he must grow up and find his place in this world which is a mixture of good and evil. Judge Cool finds both love and understanding in old age, as well as the strength to take charge of his life again, even though it means separation from his children. Dolly becomes aware that existence is more complicated than she had allowed herself to see before. Always filled with love of people, she is forced to face the reality that there is often cruelty, selfishness, and meanness in them. When she apprehends this truth, she suddenly recognizes that she is old and that her life has already been lived.

Of all the things that occur during the few days in the tree-house, the relationship that develops between Dolly and the Judge is the one the author explores most fully. Each detects in the other a correlative soul, something the Judge has searched for always. Dolly has never loved a man before, and the Judge, though he was married, was not close to his wife. He has always hoped to find "the one person in the world—from whom nothing is held back."

The Judge falls in love with Dolly and asks her to marry him, but it is too late for them. When Verena tells Dolly they have already had their lives, and that their lives have been intertwined, Dolly gives way to Verena's claim over the Judge's. Nevertheless, in the brief period of time left to Dolly, "she became what he'd wanted, the one person in the world—to whom, as he'd described it, everything can be said."

The romance between Dolly and the Judge is asexual, a daylight love; to Dolly it is an extension of the feeling she has had all her life for everyone and everything in existence. But for Judge Cool, learning about love is a process of developing and ripening. One begins with the love of something very small; that expands and becomes a link in "a chain of love" which is natural and true. Riley and Collin, who are very young, must still learn about the links of the chain. When they can do that, they will lose their loneliness and understand the significance of love.

Of the tree dwellers, Riley is the only person to have a fully developed love relationship. His courtship of Maude is described briefly, but like the comic scenes of battle, the discussion of Riley as a lover is a weak element in the novel. There is an archness and sentimentality in the description of the reformed rake's being converted by a good girl's beauty, culture, and virtue that bespeaks more of an eighteenth-century domestic novel than of a modern piece concerned in great measure with the nature of love. Capote's strength as a writer does not lie in the depiction of heterosexual love.

Other varieties of love are delineated in *The*

Grass Harp. Dolly is the recipient of many kinds of affection. Everyone cares for her, but Catherine's love for Dolly is the most moving. The bond of understanding the Judge has with Dolly is different from that of Catherine; yet Catherine is almost a part of Dolly. There is also the strangeness of Verena's attachments. Verena has cared for only two people in her life, neither of whom loved her. The first was a young woman who married a liquor salesman, leaving behind a grieving Verena. The other was Dr. Morris Ritz, who is described as a funny looking, bald-headed little man, who "looked like a mean mouse." [1] Verena was much taken with him. Nevertheless, she makes the point that she did not love Morris "in a womanly way." Her feeling for him suggests some parallels to that of Dolly and the Judge. It has no physical aspect, but is a relationship of "kindred spirits." In Verena's and Morris's case, however, Verena states it was a matter of seeing "the same devil" when they looked in each other's eyes. Soul-mates may exist for good or ill, and both Dolly and Verena find theirs. Although Dr. Ritz bilks Verena of a large sum of money, she never forgets her affection for him.

Verena's disappointment and loneliness lead her to reevaluate her relationship with her sister. When Verena comes to River Woods to see Dolly, they speak to each other for the first time as equals. Recognizing at last her need for Dolly, Verena confesses it to her. The prerogative of a lifetime with Verena is a force stronger than Dolly's new-found relationship. The Judge acknowledges that perhaps his hope to marry Dolly has all been a dream: "But a man who doesn't dream is like a man who doesn't sweat: he stores up a lot of poison."

The dream must come to an end. A great downpour of rain falls that last night. Everything seems to dissolve and be washed away. Finally, as the rain stops, a breeze comes up, and the group departs from the tree-house forever. Taking nothing with them, they leave a few possessions to rust and rot, and the woods to turn wintry. For everything there is a season, and the season in the tree-house is over.

The last brief part of the story is then told. Everyone has been affected by the events that have occurred, and each one alters his ways accordingly. Dolly, however, has reached the end of her life. Refusing to follow the doctor's orders when she develops pneumonia, she dies as she has lived. Just before she has her fatal stroke in the attic, she speaks to Collin of affection and forgiveness and the chain of love.

As in other Capote works, the last segment of the novel brings together a number of symbolic images. Rain, wind, and the suggestion of winter as the group departs from River Woods prepare the reader for the conclusion of the story. The courthouse clock strikes the nighttime hour as Dolly and Collin go up to the attic to search for silver paint. The clock will strike once again, "floating its message, each note like a banner stirring above the chilled and sleeping town," moments before Dolly collapses. Between Collin's first awareness of the striking of the clock and the second, Dolly has shown him her childhood treasures and spoken of love. While she speaks, Collin, looking at her face in the light of the oil lamp, thinks of it as a moth, "as daring, as destructible." Years before when he and Dolly first became friends the place was also the attic, and the sight of Dolly's face then was like that of a snowflake, another fragile, perishable part of nature.

The conclusion brings the work full circle. The snowflake, the moth, all the lovely delicate things must die. But at the moment of Dolly's death, at sunrise, a breeze touches the veil of her traveling hat as it is reflected in the mirror. Then Collin knows somehow that Dolly is gone, but she has passed through the town, passed the church and the hill far beyond to reach the field of Indian grass.

The grass, to which the title alludes, has a legend to it. Dolly has told Collin about the special kind of grass which she has named a "grass harp," for it knows everything about the lives of all the people. When they are dead, the grass harp remembers them, and it tells their stories. If we listen, we can hear it.

On a lovely autumn day, almost a year after Dolly's death, Collin, preparing to go north to school, takes a last walk with the Judge. They follow the route of the River Woods road, passing "the summerburned, September-burnished field." Everything is a riot of color, and as they come to the field of Indian grass Collin tells the Judge about the grass harp. Together they wait for it to sing its story.

The final passage returns to the beginning pages, a technique Capote later uses in *Breakfast at Tiffany's.* He establishes the pastness of the story about to be told. A tone of nostalgia underlies both the introduction and the conclusion, as it suggests the beauty but also the sweet melancholy of autumn with its brilliant colors and the wind blowing through the crackling leaves. Both here and in *Breakfast at Tiffany's,* the circular technique helps to create the sensation of remembrance: something lovely happened long ago and for a short time we participate in the recollection of the narrator.

Capote rewrote *The Grass Harp* for the theater. The play, produced in 1952, was far less successful than the novel had been. The dreamy poetic quality of the original did not translate well into drama. Reviewers found the play sentimental, contrived, and simplistic. Audiences apparently agreed, for it was a failure both on and off Broadway.

5

Never Love a Wild Thing:
Breakfast at Tiffany's

Like other Capote works, *Breakfast at Tiffany's,* written in 1958, received mixed notices. The same critic who said the novel was "among the best things he has written" later changed his mind and called it "slight." Another stated that the earlier fiction of Capote was "much better, truer." Yet another found something of Capote's to praise, and most readers regarded *Breakfast at Tiffany's* as the culminative effort of his daylight stories. Whatever their opinions of the merits of the work, reviewers noted certain resemblances to several Capote fictions, pointing out the kinship of Holly Golightly, the heroine, not only (as previously noted) to Miss Bobbit of "Children on Their Birthdays" but also to Joel of *Other Voices, Other Rooms* and Collin of *The Grass Harp.*[1]

Undeniably, Holly is similar in various ways to both the male and female figures of the most admired of Capote's stories: she is young and childlike, slight but attractive, friendly yet remote, her personality a touching mixture of innocence and sophistication. Like Miss Bobbit, Holly has made herself into a presence. She has deliberately created a personality to get her what she wants, and she is memorable for her own unique qualities. Furthermore, like Joel and Collin, Holly is a type of traveler. But where Joel and Collin are searching to find love and identity, Holly is

seeking experience also. She has a great hunger to
explore, to live each moment completely, to do and
see everything.

Orphaned early, Holly and her younger brother
Fred led a harsh existence in foster homes in Texas.
When they ran away, they were taken in by a kindly
horse doctor, who was widowed and the father of children older than Holly. Doc Golightly soon fell in love
with the fourteen-year-old girl and married her.
However, the marriage didn't last long. The child,
then known as Lulamae Barnes, ran off again. She as-
sumed the name and identity of Holly Golightly, big
city girl, partygoer, traveler, and lady of the evening.

All of these events took place before the beginning of the story, which is told by a writer who, like
Holly, had come to New York to seek success during
the early years of World War II.

When the story opens, the unnamed narrator has
returned to the neighborhood in which he had his first
apartment and where he had met Holly in 1943, more
than fifteen years before. At that time both are tenants in an old brownstone walk-up building, where a
fire escape takes the place of an elevator; the area is
the East Seventies near Lexington Avenue. Holly lives
in the apartment below the narrator's, and for a while
she uses him only as a "doorbell convenience," a substitute for her lost key. One night, however, when
Holly climbs the fire escape to the narrator's room to
get away from an unpleasant man in her apartment,
she and the narrator become friends.

In spite of the great differences in the way they
live, the narrator soon is Holly's confidant, but their
friendship is brief. At the end of a year, Holly flees
the United States to avoid testifying against a criminal she likes, a drug dealer named "Sally Tomato."
Because Holly has found Sally "an okay shooter,"
she makes her decision against the "badgers," apply-

ing her own code of ethics: "My yardstick," says Holly, "is how someone treats me." After instructing the narrator to find her the names of the fifty richest men in Brazil, Holly leaves the country with his help. A single postcard, without a return address, arrives from Brazil soon afterward. He never hears from her again.

Years later, the narrator comes back to his old neighborhood because he receives an excited call from Joe Bell, the bartender, who, like several other men, was devoted to Holly. Joe has been given some photographs of an African wood sculpture, which is a carved head modeled after Holly Golightly. An African tribesman was the sculptor. Little more is known of the background of the episode except that the subject of the artwork was traveling with two men in Africa, where she shared for a brief time the tribesman's hut before riding off once more. Joe Bell's call, the photographs, and the view of the brownstone in which he and Holly had lived take the narrator back in memory to his first year in New York and to reminiscences of Holly.

The story of Holly's life in New York, which has just been summarized, is now told by the narrator. He recalls Holly with tenderness, a feeling shared by Joe Bell, who speaks of his special kind of love for her. Joe's is not an erotic passion; neither is the narrator's. Both men are kind and generous to Holly, for she provokes deep affection and loyalty in them; yet, they never join the ranks of her many lovers. Her seeming helplessness, her irresponsibility, and her childlike unself-consciousness attract them as much as these qualities draw the men who provide for her financially.

In many ways Holly leads the fantasy existence children dream about. She appears to be at a continual birthday social, not only because she constantly gives or goes to parties, but also because her style of living is devoted to having fun. "I'd rob a grave. I'd

steal two-bits off a dead man's eyes if I thought it
would contribute to a day's enjoyment," says Holly.
She does whatever is necessary to maintain her way of
life. Her rules are her own, derived from a desire for
independence and the need to survive in a world she
has known to be cruel or indifferent to those who are
unprotected.

A girl of some beauty but little talent—she plays
the guitar well—Holly utilizes her looks and charm to
pay her expenses. Although she once had an opportunity to become a movie actress, she walked away
from the chance. In Hollywood she had been taken
in hand by an agent, O. J. Berman, who saw to it that
Holly was made over into starlet material. Berman
wanted to get Holly into the movies, but Holly had no
such intention. She stayed around long enough to improve her English, learn some French, and glamorize
her appearance. "I was just vamping for time to make
a few self-improvements," she tells the narrator, letting it be understood that she has not deceived herself into thinking she has talent.

Self-deception is not one of Holly's failings, although she is an extraordinary liar. It doesn't trouble
her to beguile others when it suits her purpose. She
constructs a world around her to make things as pleasant as she can, inventing stories when the truth is too
painful to discuss. Berman, who calls Holly "a phony,"
modifies it to "a *real* phony," because, he claims, "she
believes all this crap she believes." The narrator
doesn't think of Holly that way. To him she is a "lop-
sided romantic," someone "gluttonous" for life, rather
than a pretender.

Since her moral code differs from that of society,
Holly has no qualms about lying. To protect herself or
to keep people from getting too close, or from knowing too much about her, she fabricates. She fiction-
alizes when reality is grim and threatens to bring on

the "mean blues" (sadness), or the "mean reds" (fear). Unwilling to share her memories of her early life, Holly invents a beautiful fantasy childhood for herself when the narrator tells her of his own unhappy boyhood. Holly also lies when a situation is not to her liking. At a party, when an acquaintance, Mag Wildwood, barges in and draws the attention of all the men, Holly retaliates by insinuating that Mag has a terrible social disease. Another time, to keep Mag from learning that she has slept with Mag's lover, José, Holly breezily pretends she is a lesbian, partly to deceive Mag and partly for the humor of the deception.

José is no loss to Mag, though, for she gets what she really wants, marriage to Holly's millionaire playboy lover, Rusty Trawler, an unattractive, middleaged homosexual, an American fascist. He disgusts most of Holly's friends, particularly the narrator, who insists that Holly tell him how she feels about Rusty. Holly's answer is very revealing, for it encompasses an important element of her philosophy. She informs the narrator, "You can make yourself love anybody."

The idea of love keeps Holly from thinking of herself as a prostitute. She claims that she cared about all the men who paid for her favors. "I mean," she says, "you can't bang the guy and cash his checks and at least not *try* to believe you love him. I never have." Making yourself "love" anybody is what helps Holly to hold on to the way of life she has chosen. Yet, unpleasant as the idea may be, it shows Holly as existing in the same manner as Mag Wildwood, whom she detests and whom the narrator scorns. It is ironic that Mag marries Trawler, thus securing her future, but Holly is not able to follow a similar course.

Deciding to marry José, Holly chooses to ignore her relationship with Doc Golightly, claiming that the marriage could not be legal because of her age when they were wed. Because she becomes pregnant, Holly plans to go with José to Brazil, where she expects to marry him. She tells the narrator that, aside from Doc, José is her "first non-rat romance," and that she loves José. He makes her feel fine, taking away her sadness and her need for escape. The narrator notes that Holly's romance with José seems to change her. Not only does she appear content and happy, but her way of life is different also. She no longer sleeps all day and goes out all night, but instead behaves like a wife, shopping, cooking, taking José's clothes to the cleaner. Holly talks merrily of the future with José as her husband and of having many, many children.

That future never comes for Holly. José abandons Holly when her name appears in the paper as a playgirl linked with the drug ring headed by Sally Tomato. The narrator takes José's letter to Holly, who is in the hospital, having lost her baby in a scuffle with the police. When Holly sees the letter, a visible change comes over her. She seems to age and harden. She asks the narrator for her cosmetics, because "A girl doesn't read this sort of thing without her lipstick." Holly applies lipstick and rouge, eyeliner and eyeshadow, puts on pearls and dark glasses, sprays herself with perfume and lights a cigarette, readying her protective coating for what she expects to see in the letter.

The covering doesn't help. Briefly, Holly is devastated. She labels José "a rat" like all the others, although she finally agrees bitterly with the narrator that José's reasons for giving her up—his religion and his career—are valid for the kind of man he is. Holly then decides to flee the country, using the ticket for Brazil that José had bought her. Her reason for flight is not only that she wants to avoid helping the state's case against Sally; she says she'd rather the "fat woman"—that is, death—took her. Holly, with a prac-

ticality and cynicism learned early in life, knows that
the publicity she has had will be harmful to her "particular talents," and she doesn't relish trading the high
life for a marginal existence. Even though the narrator tries to dissuade her, Holly does not listen. He
argues with her, telling her she will never be able to
return to the United States, because she is under criminal indictment and will be jumping bail. A tough-
ened Holly responds: "Home is where you feel at
home. I'm still looking."

For a time it seemed that Holly had found her
dream, her "place where me and things belong together." Her relationship with José might have been
like her vision of Tiffany's, with "quietness and the
proud look of it; nothing very bad could happen to
you there." Before she met José, she had hoped that
she and her brother Fred might one day make a home
together, perhaps in Mexico, near the sea. But Fred is
killed in the war. After her bout of grief, Holly turns
to José, ready to give up her independence for the
security of belonging to someone.

Holly, however, seems fated to continue doing
what her calling card says: traveling. She has always
thought of herself, somewhat regretfully, as being like
a wild creature and feels pity for those who are attracted to the untamed. Because she is fond of Doc
Golightly, whom she left, she cautions Joe Bell, ad-
vising him never to give his heart to a wild thing:
"the more you do, the stronger they get. Until they're
strong enough to run into the woods. Or fly into a
tree. Then a taller tree. Then the sky. That's how
you'll end up. . . . If you let yourself love a wild
thing. You'll end up looking at the sky." Nevertheless, Holly knows and asserts to her friends that looking at the sky is preferable to living there, for it is
"such an empty place; so vague."

Living in the sky is the opposite of breakfasting

at Tiffany's, Holly's symbol of the good life. But there is a dichotomy in this. Holly recognizes that she must find shelter, that she cannot run all her life; yet she also wants freedom. When she buys the narrator an elegant birdcage he has admired, she makes him promise that he will "never put a living thing in it." She has an abhorrence of cages of any kind. Still Holly longs for a quiet place, somewhere to settle and make a home.

Symbolic of Holly's divided beliefs is the relationship she has with her cat, a street tom that Holly found one day near the river. Although she has looked after him lovingly for some time, as she prepares for flight to Brazil she disposes of the cat in Harlem. Both her action and her defense of it unwittingly parallel José's treatment of Holly. Her explanation to the narrator of her behavior is that she and the cat were independent, that they had no ties to one another. Having said that, Holly changes her mind and searches frantically for the cat, but she cannot find him. Filled with regret, she tells the narrator of her feelings for the cat. When the narrator promises he will find the cat and take care of him, Holly confesses her most private, deep-seated fear of what her life will always be: "Not knowing what's yours until you've thrown it away."

If Holly had found her Tiffany's, she would have given the cat a name, an indication of having roots at last; but Holly never achieves that. When they first meet, the narrator has hopes for Holly's future. Because the narrator is young and inexperienced, the older, worldly O. J. Berman disagrees with his optimism about Holly, saying, "She's strictly a girl you'll read where she ends up at the bottom of a bottle of Seconals." Years later, when Joe Bell displays the African pictures of the sculptured piece, it is apparent that Holly has never found her place, her Tiffany's, and that she is still traveling. One wonders whether she still sings the country song of years before: "Don't wanna sleep, Don't wanna die, Just wanna go a-travelin' through the pastures of the sky." The sky, however, is that lonely, empty place which both attracted and repelled Holly.

Capote once said in an interview that he had modeled Holly after a girl he had known in the early forties, and that in what he had written, "everything about her personality and her approach to life" was "literally true." Also, the prototype Holly did go to Africa. After the war, someone traveling in the Belgian Congo actually saw a wooden sculpture of her head. That, said Capote, is "all of the evidence of her existence that remains." [2]

Nevertheless, at the end of the fictional story, the narrator concludes on a more hopeful note. He tells of having seen Holly's cat one cold winter day, sitting in the window of a comfortable-looking room. Convinced that the cat has a name in that setting and a home where he now belongs, the narrator muses about Holly, the other wild thing; his words are almost an invocation as he hopes she might also have found a place for herself at last.

Much of *Breakfast at Tiffany's* is muted in tone. Although there is a great deal of humor in a number of episodes, in the dialogue, and in some of the Damon Runyonesque characters, the liveliness exists inside a frame of memory. That remembrance has, like many of Capote's stories, an autumnal sound.

Although Holly and the narrator meet in the summer, the friendship really begins in the fall, one night when "the first ripple-chills of autumn" are in the air. Over a period of a year the two become close, much as sister and brother, not as lovers. Holly even calls the narrator by her actual brother's name, Fred. Affection and understanding grow between them as

"Fred" struggles to become a successful writer and
Holly's romance with José flourishes. The next autumn,
though, brings Holly's departure and the separation
that will never be altered.

On a stormy October day, the narrator, who describes himself as "wind-blown and winded and wet
to the bone," gathers Holly's belongings together.
Carrying her rain-soaked possessions, he meets her at
Joe Bell's bar, where Joe refuses to drink to Holly's
departure. He cares too much for her and cannot bear
to see her go. As she leaves, Joe thrusts a bunch of
flowers at Holly, but, emblematically, they fall to the
floor. The wind whips through the streets as the narrator and Holly go towards the airport. And Holly is
gone.

Years later, when the narrator, now a famous
writer, returns to the old neighborhood, it is once
again October, a season of haziness and memory. He
comes back in a downpour of rain, an afternoon which
reminds one of the day of Holly's departure. It suggests the end of a cycle, the days of the past, which
"blow about in memory, lazy, autumnal, all alike as
leaves"; and now there is the waning day, the fallen
leaves yellowed, covering the pavement, wet and slip-
pery from the rain. The mist in the air touches everything, creating a sense of loneliness.

Breakfast at Tiffany's goes full circle. The beginning, which is actually the ending, has a gentle feeling of nostalgia. One hears in the background the
echo of "gone" and "was," from *Other Voices, Other
Rooms,* as the narrator walks towards the old brownstone apartment house, which stands "next to a church
where a blue tower-clock tells the hours." This use of
the past, memory, and sweet sadness is an identifying
element of Capote's style. It is what some critics object to, labeling it style without substance. But this
seems unfair caviling. For it is just that characteristic

which sets off the story, encloses it, as if it were a
narrative scene inside a crystal paperweight.[3] At the
same time that it pleases and delights, it suggests
something else, a pleasurable melancholy for the days
that are no more.[4]

6

Surprised by Joy:
Stories of the
Fifties and Sixties

The story "A Diamond Guitar," which appeared first
in *Harper's Bazaar* in 1950, was reprinted in the collection Capote called *Breakfast at Tiffany's: A Short
Novel and Three Short Stories,* in 1958. Also included
in the group were "A House of Flowers" (1951) and
"A Christmas Memory" (1956), both of which had
been published in *Mademoiselle*. The story, "Among
the Paths to Eden" (1960), printed originally in *Esquire,* is in *Selected Writings* (1963), which also contains a reissue of *Breakfast at Tiffany's*.

"A Diamond Guitar" reveals Capote's early interest in prison stories as well as his sympathy towards
certain kinds of convicts. The same empathy exists in
the book *In Cold Blood* and in his collaborative writing of the script for a prison movie, *The Glass House*.

The setting of "A Diamond Guitar" is a Southern
prison farm twenty miles from the closest town. It is
a different kind of prison, located in a pine forest from
which the prisoners take turpentine. Unlike city penal
institutions there are few reminders of physical re-
strictions. A red clay road leads to the prison in the
pines. At night the men can go into the yard to look
up at the stars, or go to sleep with moonlight coming
through the windows. There is a great stillness in this
prison story, but it is the quiet that comes with the
absence of life. Although the convicts live in a nat-

ural environment, they are as unhappy as any people who live behind bars. Some chafe for the real world, whatever that is for each of them; others have blocked out all hope of change, living only in the present. Mr. Schaeffer, the major figure in the story, is one of the latter.

Mr. Schaeffer has been sentenced to life imprisonment for killing a "man [who] deserved to die." At fifty he has been in prison for seventeen years. A lonely man, with no friends outside the prison and no close friends inside, he is one of the few convicts who can read and write, and he helps other prisoners when possible. He is also a carver who makes dolls that are sold in town, a talent that provides Mr. Schaeffer with small sums of money.

One day a young Cuban named Tico Feo is brought into the prison and assigned to Schaeffer, who is to teach him the routine. Schaeffer is very much taken with the golden-haired, blue-eyed boy who plays a jeweled guitar. Tico Feo makes him feel alive, and he remembers the pleasures as well as the pain of what life once was. Schaeffer "had not wanted to be alive," but he and all the prisoners are affected by the presence of Tico Feo. When he plays his guitar the prisoners sing and dance and laugh as they had not before he came.

The two men become good friends when Schaeffer gives Tico Feo dolls for his sisters. The older man is generous to the younger, sharing with him the things he gets from his earnings. Although Schaeffer knows that Tico Feo lies and is lazy, he tells himself that Tico Feo is a boy and "it will be a long time" before he is a grown-up. He thus forgives him for his untruths and exaggerations.

But Tico Feo arouses a great feeling of sadness in the men, emotion brought on by his music, which revives memories of life outside the prison walls. Schaeffer's emotional barriers are broken down by his closeness to the boy, and although there is no sexual relationship, "they were as lovers."

The young man does not adjust to the penal life. He constantly speaks of the freedoms of the real world. However, the outside world evoked for Mr. Schaeffer is different from what Tico Feo represents. Mr. Schaeffer reawakens to dreams of brown rivers and sunlight, but Tico Feo's "El Mundo" is gaudy and artificial, like the glass-diamonded guitar.

Tico Feo wants to escape from the prison. Although Schaeffer believes himself too old to begin a totally new life, Tico Feo finally persuades the man to break out with him. One day, during a time the convicts are at work in the forest, the two men attempt to escape. However, as Schaeffer is running he trips over a log in the creek, breaking his ankle. As he looks up at Tico Feo's face, he realizes that the boy "had not wanted him to make it, had never thought he would." In addition to being a liar and a thief, the young prisoner is also a betrayer. Schaeffer remembers how he had thought "it would be a long time before his friend was a grown man."

The guards find Schaeffer but Tico Feo escapes and is never found. The Captain of the prison protects Schaeffer by claiming he had attempted to prevent Tico Feo from escaping.

Schaeffer is left with a limp and Tico Feo's guitar, for there is nobody who can play it properly. As the years pass, the glass diamonds turn yellow. Sometimes during the long nights Mr. Schaeffer's fingers "drift across the strings: then, the world." Where he had shut out the world before he met Tico Feo, he can do that no longer. Once he had chosen not to be alive, for to be numb was to be free from pain; Mr.

Schaeffer's discovery of love has now made him a vulnerable man. Lonelier than ever, he remembers, he
dreams, and he suffers.

One of the many places to which Tico Feo had
sailed before his imprisonment was Haiti, the island
setting for Capote's story, "House of Flowers." It begins in Port-au-Prince, the seaport capital of Haiti,
the city to which Ottilie, the central figure in the
story, walked from her mountain home three years
earlier.[1] She remains in Port-au-Prince until she meets
a handsome young man, Royal Bonaparte, marries,
and goes to live with him in his home high up in the
mountains.

Ottilie is a beautiful seventeen-year-old of mixed
parentage. When Ottilie was a child her mother died,
and her father, a planter, returned to France. Brought
up by a coarse peasant family, whose sons all used her
sexually, Ottilie slips easily into the life of a prostitute
when she is befriended by a kind man in the market-
place of Port-au-Prince. He takes her to his cousin who
runs an establishment known as the Champs Elysées.
It is a narrow old building covered with bougainvillea
vines, a house of many balconies and a porch where
the eight resident prostitutes sit in the evening fanning themselves and telling stories.

Delighted with her good luck, paid for doing
what was previously one of her household chores, Ottilie revels in her success: five dresses made of silk,
green satin shoes, three gold teeth valued at thou-
sands of francs, steady customers for her services, and
an armful of gold bracelets given to her by an admirer,
a middle-aged American engineer named Mr. Jamison. Ottilie marvels at the juke box and the electric
light and thinks very seldom of the mountain area
that had been her home.

Yet, with all her pleasures, she has a feeling of
discontent. When her friends, Baby and Rosita, speak

of the bliss of love, Ottilie realizes that she has never known it. Disturbed by this, she goes to a *Houngan*, a voodooist, to find out about the secret of love. When she can hold a bee in her hand without being stung, she is told, then she will know she has found love. Wondering whether she might be in love with Mr. Jamison, Ottilie tries out the message of the gods. When she catches a black bee in her hands she is stung.

Then at carnival time Ottilie goes to a cockfight, where she sees a ginger-colored, smooth and shiny-skinned man, his appearance as arrogant as the cock he has brought to the match. Ottilie feels she has "never known anyone so beautiful." The man, Royal, and Ottilie dance and talk, and Ottilie finds herself comfortable with Royal, "for the mountains were still with her, and he was of the mountains." They go into a wooded area, where they make love. Afterwards, as Royal lies on the ground asleep, Ottilie catches a bee. When the bee fails to sting her, she understands that she is in love at last.

They go to Royal's mountain home which is "like a house of flowers," perched far above the sea. Wisteria covers the roof, vines hang over the windows, lilies grow near the doorway. There in the one-room house Ottilie lives joyfully, except for two problems. One is that Royal after a few months returns to some of his bachelor habits. However, Ottilie manages to accept this. But she is tormented by the other obstacle to her happiness, Royal's grandmother, Old Bonaparte.

The old woman is very cruel to Ottilie, pinching her and predicting an early death for her. People for miles around, and Royal as well, are afraid of Old Bonaparte's power to make spells. At night, when Ottilie and Royal make love, she thinks the grandmother is watching them, and once she is certain she sees a "gummy" eye staring at her in the dark. When Ottilie begins to find strange things in her sewing basket—a cat's head, a snake, spiders, a lizard, a buzzard's breast—she realizes that Old Bonaparte is trying to put a curse on her. Ottilie says nothing, but each day she cooks into the old woman's food the animal parts she finds. When at last Ottilie tells the grandmother what she has done, the old lady collapses and dies.

Not long after the grandmother's death, Ottilie begins to think she is being haunted. One night when she sees an eye staring at her in the dark, she tells Royal what had happened. When she asks him whether she had done wrong he cannot judge, but he decides that Ottilie must be punished to appease the old woman's ghost. Only then will Ottilie be left in peace.

Royal ties Ottilie to a tree in the yard and goes off to work. As she dozes she is amazed to see her two friends, Baby and Rosita, coming up the path. Ottilie's old admirer, Mr. Jamison, provided a car for them to find out what had happened to Ottilie. When the women untie Ottilie, they go into the house, where she puts on a silk dress and stockings and pearl earrings. The three of them drink rum all day and tell stories. Ottilie is happy in her friends' company, but when they expect her to leave with them she is startled, for she has no intention of deserting Royal. Baby and Rosita tie Ottilie up again in the yard once they realize she loves her husband. They return to Port-au-Prince to announce that Ottilie is dead.

As twilight settles in, Ottilie, hearing Royal's footsteps, throws herself into a position suggesting she has met with violence, happily planning to give "a good scare" to Royal. With that scene the story concludes. Ottilie has done her penance; Royal does his when he is frightened by the way his wife looks as he comes towards the house. But as in any fairy tale, all's well that ends well.

In looking at "House of Flowers" the reader may readily see why Capote used it as the basis for the musical comedy which he wrote in 1954. The story has many of the characteristics of the genre: lightness, humor, exotic setting, and one-dimensional characters. As fiction, the work is a loose mixture of love story and violence; neither part is memorable. The strangeness of the setting does not alter the superficiality of the romantic tale. And the introduction of voodoo, the evil eye, cockfights, superstition, wizardry, and death is more humorous than serious. Where Capote has used similar elements at other times to provide a look at the dark side of human nature, in "House of Flowers" they seem merely colorful.

Capote's ability to combine comedy, nostalgia, and a child's sense of tragedy is nowhere more evident than in the story "A Christmas Memory." Declared by Capote to be his most cherished piece, it is more overtly autobiographical than anything else he has written. The author has said that the child in the story is himself and the elderly relative, his cousin, Miss Sook Faulk. He further emphasized the reality behind the fiction in "A Christmas Memory" by having a childhood picture of himself and Miss Faulk reproduced for a reprinting of the story in 1966, ten years after its original publication.

In addition to seeing the autobiographical connection between the story and the author, the reader can discern immediately similarities to Capote's novel, *The Grass Harp*. In both works, the major figures are a young boy and his older female relative; the scenes take place primarily in the kitchen and in the woods; the story is set in the past and the tone is nostalgic; and an event of great significance takes place in both

the story and the novel, that is, the parting of the
child and his cousin. In *The Grass Harp* the woman
dies and the young man goes north to school, whereas
in "A Christmas Memory" the boy is sent away to
a military school, never to see his cousin again; her
death occurs after his leaving.

"A Christmas Memory" opens as the narrator
evokes memories of late November mornings spent in
a warm country kitchen. Looking backwards the
speaker becomes a seven-year-old who has lived for a
long time with his distant cousin. Although it is not
her house, in his child's world the other inhabitants
don't matter unless they cause difficulties. The old
woman and the boy, whom she has named Buddy,
after a childhood friend of hers who died in the
1880s,[2] are best friends. It is possible because the
white-haired, small, sprightly, craggy yet delicate-
faced woman with sherry-colored, timid eyes has
never outgrown the sunny world of childhood. Buddy
stresses the great difference between her and others,
saying, "She is still a child."

On a particular morning every November, a special ritual is repeated. His cousin looks out the window, notes the chill of the season, thinks of Christmas, and makes the pronouncement: "It's fruitcake
weather." The two of them find her hat—worn more
for propriety than for warmth, a straw cartwheel decorated with roses of velvet—and get Buddy's old baby
carriage, which serves as a cart for carrying the load
of pecans that will go into the fruitcake. Along with
their dog, Queenie, they walk to a pecan grove,
where, on their hands and knees, for hours they will
search out nuts.

Their expeditions are like those in *The Grass
Harp*. Dolly, Catherine, and Collin go to the woods
to gather ingredients for Dolly's dropsy medicine or
to picnic. Buddy and his cousin collect flowers, herbs,

and ferns in the spring, firewood in the winter, and
fish the creek in the summer. The lives of the two families resemble each other in their patterns. And another similarity exists in their attitudes toward money.
It is intended to bring pleasure. However, where
Dolly, Catherine, and Collin have Dolly's earnings to
purchase magazines and games, Buddy and his cousin
enter contests to try to win money to support their
activities; they also sell jars of jams, jellies, and pre-
serves they've made, berries they've gathered, and
flowers they've picked for important occasions.

They need money for the buying of the items
that go into the fruitcake, the candied fruits, the
spices, the whiskey, the flour, the butter, the eggs.
All year long they save in their "Fruitcake Fund;"
most of it is in pennies, which they count out for the
thirty or more cakes they send to people they like,
such as President Roosevelt, a bus driver who waves
at them every day, and a couple who once took a picture of them. And afterwards there are the thank-you
letters for their scrapbooks.

The fun and excitement of shopping is followed
by the pleasure of preparing the cakes: the glowing
of the stove, the sounds of the mixing, the smells of
the spices delight Buddy. However, in four days it is
all over and he feels let down afterwards. His cousin
has a remedy though for depression, the whiskey left
from the baking. After Queenie gets a spoonful mixed
in coffee, the two of them drink the remainder. Then
the sour taste of the liquor is soon replaced by happy
feelings. They begin to giggle, to sing, and to dance.
Queenie rolls in drunken joy as the cousin waltzes
around in her squeaky tennis shoes.

The delightful comedy of the drinking scene is
produced by the deft touch of the writer, not only
here but elsewhere in the work as well. The description of the meeting with Haha Jones—so named for

his somber disposition—proprietor of the shop where they buy the whiskey for the cakes, is another episode enlivened by the lightness of the humor. Looking at the odd pair, Haha asks, "Which one of you is a drinking man?" The appearance of Haha and the tongue-in-cheek designation of the "sinful" café he runs all add to the comic note.

There are also other kinds of humor in the story. A line here and there suggests the eighteenth-century satirist Alexander Pope. When the narrator tells of earning pennies by killing house flies, he says in mock-heroic style, "Oh the carnage of August: the flies that flew to heaven!" Superstition further provides the opportunity for comedy; the number thirteen has several possibilities. Fear of having thirteen dollars causes Buddy and his cousin to throw a penny out of the window to avoid the multiple catastrophes that could occur from the unlucky sum. Twelve ninety-nine is safer. The importance of hoarding the money of the "Fund" provides another chance for verbal and visual humor. Buddy makes the following statement, creating an expanding comic effect by the use of detail and the repetition of the word "under": "These moneys we keep hidden in an ancient purse under a loose board under the floor under a chamber pot under my friend's bed."

The only money ever withdrawn from their savings is the ten cents Buddy is given each week for the movies, to which he goes alone. Although his elderly cousin enjoys hearing him tell the film story, she has never been to a movie. Her life, like that of Dolly Talbo, is that of a recluse. One thinks of Dolly's nunlike, pink room when Buddy describes his cousin's bedroom containing an iron bed painted in her favorite rose pink. Further, his cousin has never been far from home, has had very limited experiences, and is ignorant of the world outside the little town in which she lives. Yet she knows all kinds of wonderful things a small boy admires: how to tame hummingbirds, how to tell terrifying ghost stories, and how to treat ailments by using old Indian cures.

Buddy's cousin, who reads only the funny papers and the Bible, is a religious Christian who fully expects to come face to face with God at the end of her life. However, she also understands the natural world, loves and respects it. Once someone chides her for refusing to sell a beautiful fragrant pine she has cut for a Christmas tree and she is told she can get another one. But she responds like a nineteenth-century Romantic philosopher in tune with nature: "There's never two of anything."

Decorating the Christmas tree they have dragged home from the woods and making presents consumes much of their time. As early as August they pick cotton to sprinkle on the tree in December. Later, old treasures are brought down from the attic; cutouts of fruits and animals are made from colored paper and tinfoil angels from candy wrappers. They make holly wreaths and family gifts together. But then they separate to make the most important items, the things they will exchange with each other. Both want to give something special, but they have no money for bought presents. Because of that, every year they design colorful handmade kites.

When the holidays are over and the wind is right, they go out of doors to the nearby pastures to fly their kites. Thus the seasons pass, from fruitcake time to tree cutting and decorating, to kite-flying weather. And during the last kite-flying days they have together, Buddy's cousin speaks of a sudden vision she has. She tells him that God shows Himself in many guises, but only at the end of life do we realize that He "has already shown Himself." And as she says that to Buddy, she moves her hand in an encompassing gesture "that gathers clouds and kites and grass and Queenie pawing earth over her bone."

It is not long after his cousin has described to him her sense of a godlike indwelling that Buddy is parted from her. He is forced to take up a new life in military schools, camps, and another home. However, because of his love for his cousin and his great sense of loss in the separation, he never feels that he belongs anywhere. He always identifies home with his cousin.

Remaining alone, his cousin writes him of her activities and sorrows, of the death of Queenie. Each November she sends him the best of the fruitcakes. But she lives only a few years more. Soon her memory fails and she can no longer distinguish the narrator from the Buddy who was her childhood friend.

In the winter season when she dies, Buddy intuits her death before he is told of it. He describes his feeling of loss as an "irreplaceable part" of himself, "loose like a kite on a broken string." He looks up to the December sky as if to see that lost self of his joining with his other self, the spirit of his cousin, "rather like hearts, a lost pair of kites hurrying toward heaven."

The concluding passage in its nostalgia and tenderness hearkens back to the last section of *The Grass Harp*, in which Collin becomes aware of Dolly's spirit moving from the confined world of human existence to the eternal freedom of nature, symbolized by the Indian grass which is the Grass Harp. The conclusion of the story differs, however, from that of the novel in one significant aspect: Collin accepts Dolly's death, seeing it as a part of the mortal cycle, the human story, and recognizes that he must move on. Buddy, on the other hand, has a sense of irrevocable loss; the perception is reinforced by the words "irreplaceable," "broken," "searching," and "lost." Dolly's presence seems to continue in nature, in the singing grass, but Buddy's cousin has gone far beyond the wintry sky.

"The Thanksgiving Visitor" was published in 1967, following the reissue of "A Christmas Memory." In numerous ways the two stories can be paired: the time period is the same, 1932–34, and the place is rural Alabama; the major characters are Buddy and his elderly cousin; their way of life and their activities follow a similar pattern. But there are also important differences. "The Thanksgiving Visitor" is more specifically detailed and less sentimental than the earlier work. However, it lacks the tenderness as well as the humor of "A Christmas Memory." The poetic quality is gone as well as the nostalgia. It is as though the author, having come to terms with the anger and pain of his childhood, looks back more objectively to those years that he retraces in both stories.

The elderly cousin, known only as "my friend" in "A Christmas Memory," is now given her actual name, Miss Sook Faulk. Her character and personality once again are central to the theme. Buddy learns a significant lesson about kindness from Miss Sook, one that he grows to understand eventually. The plot of the story is built on the gentle moral teaching of the lady.

I was "a sissy of sorts," says the grown-up Buddy, looking back at himself as a small child in second grade. Although Buddy doesn't object to being educated, he fears going to school because of an older boy in his class, Odd Henderson. Odd is a big, rambunctious twelve-year-old who terrifies all the children, even those his own age. Buddy is so frightened of Odd that he tries to avoid attending school. He has nightmares because he feels tormented by Odd. However, when he tells Miss Sook about it, Buddy is distressed by her unwillingness to condemn Odd. In-

stead, his cousin is sympathetic toward Odd, saying
he is to be pitied because of his hard life and disreputable father.

Odd's father, Dad Henderson, a bootlegger who
spends most of his days in jail, is married to a woman
Miss Sook remembers fondly. Molly Henderson, much
younger than her husband, was once a red-haired,
lovely girl. But now, says Miss Sook, she has become
a toothless hag at thirty-five, with no money and "a
houseful of children to feed."

Miss Sook expects Buddy to have tolerance and
pity, for the two of them agree on everything else.
Thus, when she wants to invite Odd Henderson for
Thanksgiving dinner, she assumes Buddy will agree
with her decision. He doesn't; but his cousin goes to
the Henderson home anyway to issue an invitation.
She returns, filled with sadness by the poverty she has
witnessed, telling Buddy of "the shame" she feels "for
all of us who have anything extra when other people
have nothing."

To Buddy's dismay, Odd comes to the Faulk
house for Thanksgiving dinner. But neither of the
boys gets to sample the feast of glazed turkey, am-
brosia, whipped sweet potatoes, fritters, mince pie, or
banana pudding—Buddy's favorite dish. After grace
has been recited and as the thirty people prepare to
eat dinner, Buddy accuses Odd of having stolen Miss
Sook's cameo from her bureau. Although it is true,
Miss Sook denies it, attempting to protect Odd Henderson. She says that Buddy has been playing a joke.
With that, Buddy's uncle insists that he apologize.
But Odd Henderson does not allow it. He confesses
and leaves, after saying, "You must be a special lady,
Miss Sook, to fib for me like that."

Buddy runs out of the house, taking shelter in a
nearby smokehouse. There, late in the afternoon, Miss
Sook finds him. Despite his self-pity, Buddy accepts

the turkey leg his cousin has brought him. And he listens to her, although he scarcely understands what she tells him about wrongdoing. Only "deliberate cruelty" is "unpardonable," says Miss Faulk, as she attempts to explain that Odd's action though wrong was not calculated. Buddy's behavior, however, was inexcusable because it was an intentional wrong. The adult narrator Buddy notes that he learned after a period of time the significance of the event. But what immediately concerns the child Buddy is the assurance of the continuing love and friendship of his cousin. She convinces him he can never lose those.

Odd Henderson never bothers Buddy again. Soon Odd leaves school to work on a dairy farm, and eventually he goes away to join the Merchant Marine. The last time Buddy sees Odd is in the Faulk garden. Miss Sook and Buddy have been trying to move a large pot of chrysanthemums, when Odd Henderson comes along and carries the heavy tub for Miss Sook. Thanking him for his neighborliness, she cuts a large bouquet of flowers for Odd's mother, sending it with her love. Odd leaves as Miss Sook calls after him, and the story comes to an end.

In "A Thanksgiving Visitor" the reader has little of the sense of loneliness or isolation so prevalent in *The Grass Harp* and "A Christmas Memory." In those stories the boy seems to be separated from ordinary life and other people, so that there appears to be a feeling of distance. The child in "A Thanksgiving Visitor," however, leads an everyday existence. In all three stories there are other family members, but in *The Grass Harp* and "A Christmas Memory" they are regarded as enemies, outside the closed circle. In "A Thanksgiving Visitor" Miss Sook has two sisters, "vaguely masculine ladies" who are involved in numerous businesses. The sisters aren't named and play no real part in the story; but Uncle B., Miss Sook's brother, now seen as a kind but silent man, is an integral part of Buddy's life. His is "the deciding voice in the house"; he is the head of the family; it is for him that enormous meals are prepared by Miss Sook; he is the one who slaughters the animals or poultry and thinks Buddy needs to learn to do such things also; and he is the person who wants Buddy to have friends other than Miss Sook, male friends.

The description of life during Depression times in the rural South, of Buddy's relatives and the interplay between characters, creates a story very different in tonal quality and imagery from "A Christmas Memory." In making daily events in the Faulk household run a rather ordinary course and in creating a moral end for the Thanksgiving story, the writer loses a certain quality that is an animating force in the earlier story: delicacy and freshness and a glimmer of a past that can never be brought back. "A Christmas Memory" tells only what one needs to know. Anything else is superfluous.

"Among the Paths to Eden" reveals a different side of Capote. In this story his characters are middle-aged; the time is the present; the setting is realistic; the pace is brisk. Told in third-person narrative, the work reveals an attitude of sympathy but not sentiment towards the protagonists. Although the two people in the story are shown somewhat ironically, the humor contains warmth and an understanding of human frailties.

One pleasant March day, Ivor Belli, a fifty-five-year-old widower, decides to visit his wife's grave, something he has not done since her burial in the fall. Neither affection nor a sense of loss prompts the action. Mr. Belli, far from being unhappy, is enjoying his bachelor life. However, the harsh winter has just come to an end, and Mr. Belli, responding to the hint of spring in the air, wants to get out-of-doors for a

walk. A trip to the cemetery will provide him with a
stroll in the sunshine and will also mollify one of his
daughters.

Taking a bouquet of jonquils with him, Mr. Belli
sets out with a feeling of joie de vivre. That changes
when he arrives at the huge, ugly cemetery in Queens
where his wife is buried. Suddenly, as he hurries to
reach his wife's grave, the day seems chill, "the sunshine . . . false, without real warmth." Mr. Belli has
anticipated "the aroma of another spring about to be,"
but instead he has been reminded of his own mortality. Anxious to be on his way, Mr. Belli hastily pushes
the jonquils into an urn on the tomb. Yet, he pauses
to prune the flowers, regretting that "he could not
delay their doom by supplying them with water."

The jonquils, first flowers after a dead season,
March and its promise of happiness, the quiet graves,
the sun and winds which first seem warm and then
turn cold are vital parts of the theme, and their significance becomes apparent as the story progresses.

As Mr. Belli turns to leave the gravesite, he encounters a woman standing nearby. Although she
speaks to him sympathetically, she appears strangely
gratified that the dead relative is Mr. Belli's wife. The
woman, Mary O'Meaghan, is a reader of obituary col-
umns. Following the advice of a friend, Mary fre-
quents the cemetery in hope of meeting a lonely widower who wants to marry again. She confesses this to
Belli later, only after he tells her he would never
consider marriage another time.

Mary had looked after her father until he died,
and she has been left with nothing to do. She is "on
the right side of forty," heavy, bespectacled, drab
looking in spite of her healthy coloring; her finger-
nails are bitten, and she wears orthopedic shoes because of a game leg. Possessing only the skills of cooking and taking care of people, Mary feels there is

nothing in life for her except marriage. Nevertheless, all her ventures are fruitless.

The effect Mary has on Belli, however, is a positive one, though not for her. Mary's appearance, Mr. Belli decides, is that of a "decent-looking person," the kind "you could trust." When he comes to that conclusion, Mr. Belli immediately thinks of his secretary, Miss Jackson, a pleasant, good-natured woman, whom "lately, absentmindedly" he'd been calling by her first name, Esther. Mary has no idea of the direction Mr. Belli's thoughts take as a result of their meeting.

Knowing that she must hold Belli's attention, Mary offers him peanuts—it is lunchtime—and quickly launches into a discussion of food, for cooking is her strong suit. As they sit on his wife's grave, Belli's mood softens. Mary suggests that he must miss his wife's cooking, and Belli remembers the better aspects of his marriage: the good meals, "the cinnamon-scented feastdays," the "afternoons of gravy and wine," his pleasure in the fresh linen and silver. Having thought for so long only of his wife's nagging, Belli happily recalls her virtues as wife and mother. He wishes that he had brought an orchid to her grave, a flower she cherished.

When Mary flatters Belli, telling him he looks too young to be a grandfather, the compliment has a magical effect. He feels young again, rejuvenated. The mood with which he first started out the day is recaptured, "perhaps . . . because the wind had subsided, the warmth of the sun grown more authentic." Once more he has the feeling of immortality. A season lies before him.

The beauty of the day prompts Mary to speak of parades and of music and singers, especially of Helen Morgan, whom Belli had "truly" loved. When Mary begins to sing it is a perfect imitation of Helen Morgan's voice. Soon Mary seems to become a differ-

ent person, with "a natural expression of some se-
cluded identity." While she is singing, a Negro funeral
procession interrupts them. Mary is embarrased, apologetic, but Belli praises her, asking for an encore. Her
response is like that of "a child to whom he'd handed
a balloon" which carried her through the air. Full of
happiness Mary promises she will sing for him again
if he will come to dinner.

The invitation destroys the atmosphere she has
created, and Belli sees her once again as she is. Con-
firmed in his suspicion that Mary is a husband hunter,
he gives one evasive answer after another to her, until she asks directly about marrying. Belli tells Mary
that "twenty-seven years" of marriage were "enough
for any lifetime."

Although Mary's hopes for a future with Belli are
shattered, she does not give up the idea of finding
a husband among the mourners in the cemetery. As
the two walk to the gate, a "new pilgrim" enters, at-
tracting Mary's attention, a lively "little man" of
"cheery whistlings and . . . plenty of snap to his walk."
When Belli sees the man and notes Mary's interest, he
wishes her luck and thanks her for the peanuts.

Mary's desire to find happiness, or Eden, with
Belli cannot be fulfilled, but she has served as the
catalyst for the rebirth of feeling in him. The vague
stirrings that he has when he first meets her and is
reminded of Esther Jackson build throughout the time
they spend together. At the moment Belli declares to
Mary that he has had enough years of marriage, he
comes to a decision that he will marry Esther Jackson
in April or May. First he will take her for dinner and
bowling, and he will buy her an "orchid, a gala purple
one with a lavender-ribbon bow."

The orchid represents not only another beginning for Belli in a fresh season but also an acceptance
of that which was good in the season that has gone.

Throughout the story there is a play on mortality-im-
mortality. Man's life is like a flower, like the seasons;
the warmth and chill of the sun and wind remind him
of his days. And surely, Capote's most ironic use of
the theme appears in the discovery of love in a cemetery. Eden as everlasting life, a paradise of eternal
youth, is the path Belli seeks among the quiet graves.

"Among the Paths to Eden" must be counted as
one of Capote's best stories. The humor, intriguing
story line, and personalities of the characters all mesh
under the controlled pen of the writer.[3] It is one of a
kind. Capote's later work bears no resemblances to
"Among the Paths to Eden."

7

People, Places, and the Celebrity Life: The Nonfiction Pieces

Local Color is a collection of nine unrelated sketches that Capote wrote for various magazines between 1946 and 1950. They consist of observations and stories about places he has lived and visited and some of the people he has met in his travels. In a later work, *The Dogs Bark*, published in 1973, Capote included *Local Color*. However, the 1950 edition is more interesting than the 1973 reprint, because it contains an impressive group of photographs which create not only meaning in themselves but also significant interpretations of the prose. Capote's use of pictures by a variety of well-known artists indicates his sensitivity to the medium, and, not surprisingly, he was to write the commentary for Richard Avedon's collection of photographs, *Observations,* in 1959.

Each sketch has a photograph as introduction and one at the conclusion. In the opening piece, "New Orleans," both pictures focus on the architecture of the city. The first shows an elderly woman walking with a cane beneath a beautiful, elaborately wrought balcony typical of New Orleans. The second is a long shot of a street, stressing its narrowness. All along the avenue pillars hold up the intricately designed balconies.

Capote begins by talking about the "old white

rooms" in which he stays, rooms that, with their high, carved ceilings, French windows, and wide doors, remind the reader of Southern plays. In the courtyard stands a statue, an angel of black stone.

New Orleans has different moods. During the summer the author hears conversations of families, sounds of a mother singing to her baby. He watches a foreign woman plucking a chicken on her balcony and letting the feathers float away.

One cold Sunday morning in winter he takes a walk to the Quarter, where he wants to buy fruit and winter flowers. Out of impulse he detours into a courtyard. It is an upsetting experience, for he sees a man who has hanged himself from a willow tree. There is a fountain sculpture of a monkey with water spouting from its mouth, and the water makes "desolate bell-like sounds" as it falls on pool pebbles. Feeling the "terror" of the "silent suffocated garden," he looks at the body swinging in sun and shadow. He wonders if the man has killed himself for love, and he runs from the quiet courtyard.

New Orleans is a shabby city, he states, "like every southern town . . . a city of soft-drink signs." Torn posters and fragments of paper are everywhere, advertisements of every kind, not only touting beverages, but also giving warnings, notices, and invitations.

The people he describes all add to the sense of the decay of the city. There is the unimaginative proprietress of an empty cafe, who has the same sign hanging in seven places over the bar; and a woman, who invites him to call, lives in a shabby neighborhood in a deteriorating house, which inside still reflects the long-ago world of crystal and carved furniture. He has an elderly neighbor, who plays the banjo, drum, and harmonica, a man who is disreputable in every way but who always has some woman looking after him. Capote calls him a "dissipated satyr." The last time he sees the man is in his bedroom, where the man has sneaked in to steal Capote's box of pennies.

One Saturday night Capote goes to a Negro cafe, where he listens to Shotgun, the entertainer, sing and play the piano.[1] Shotgun has a "wicked red tongue," that tastes "the tune, loving it, making love to it." Capote muses, "Is there any human vice he doesn't know about?" It's too bad, he thinks, that few white people hear Shotgun. The nightclub for a short time seems to him the world in little, where everything exists inside the "dark, jazzy, terrible room."

Capote's reactions to the nightclub seem to mirror what he has been describing throughout the piece: the warmth and cold; the sweetness and horror; the shabbiness, the decay, and the energy; pleasure and desire, all that we yearn for.

The loneliness of life in the city is the theme of the second work in the book. "New York," which is "like a diamond iceberg," is a city of lost dreams, even for the rich and famous.

In his childhood Capote had been an admirer of Greta Garbo, and once he had sent her a copy of a play he'd written. When she failed to respond, he felt very angry. But when he sees Garbo in New York, twice in one week, once at the movies and once at an antique shop, his earlier admiration for her revives. Miss Garbo's beauty is overwhelming; yet he has a sense of the tragic element in her.

At another time he meets a woman friend who has not succeeded as a poet and is down on her luck. He advises her to go home to her family. However, her situation causes him to think of New York as a trap for "the talented untalented," the people who belong neither in their provincial home towns nor in the art capital. He blames the problem on American attitudes of not valuing anything that fails to bring a cash return.

The idea of lost dreams is continued in the story of Joe Vitale, a middle-aged radio repairman, who once had been a lifeguard and champion swimmer. Vitale puts notices in the window of his shop, announcing his intention to swim from Rockaway Beach to Jones Beach one August day. However, Joe Vitale's dream is not realized, although briefly he gains fame with stories and pictures of his attempt. When Vitale tries to swim in the ocean, lifeguards force him back to shore. The accounts in the newspapers turn him into the figure of a fool, says Capote with gentleness and empathy. Like Prufrock, Vitale cannot hear the mermaids singing. Wanting to tell Vitale how much he thinks of him, Capote goes to the shop. But it is closed, and Vitale is gone.

When a friend, Hilary, invites him for tea, Capote thinks about Hilary's skill in being able to transform ordinary human beings into creatures of glamor. He has the effect of making people feel good by persuading them that they are special, unique. Hilary has the ability to relieve a friend's sorrow, and the writer believes that Hilary feels the pain of others intensely. Still, Capote dreads the possibility that Hilary might one day discover that not everyone loves him.

One hot August day, drained and exhausted, Capote tells himself it would be much better for him if he were to leave New York. The city is a colossal time waster. Work would improve elsewhere. In New York one is always restless, searching.

When his birthday comes, he hears from his oldest friend, Selma, a woman of eighty-three. She once worked as a cook for his aunts in Alabama. As a boy, when he was leaving Alabama, he had wanted Selma to take the trip with him, but she was frightened and wouldn't go. At first he was lonely, an unhappy lost boy. Soon, however, he began to think of all the things he was seeing and started to invent stories about them, saving them up to tell Selma. But as he stored things, they changed from reality to something different and, in time, only the "echo of haunting wonder" remained.

The photographs that accompany "New York" depict both the beauty and the isolation of the city. The first is a scene of the ferry moving towards the shoreline. Beyond is the magnificent New York skyline. The second picture has a surrealistic effect. It is composed of an elongated shadow of a man and a foreshortened shadow of a building. Both have an anonymity that is disturbing, and there is neither ground below nor sky above. Through his comments and vignettes, Capote shows a city as the iceberg he has called it. It is a place of indifferent cruelty. People are drawn to New York; it glitters and beckons; it seems to promise happiness, but in reality it is a great machine which devours people.

"Brooklyn" tells of decay. Although the name of the borough provokes laughter in many people, who associate it with poor speech and dress and bad manners, Capote thinks of it as a lonely place where all the people seem lost.

He lives for awhile in a dark, grimy Victorian brownstone, run by a woman and her daughter. To support themselves, the two have an answering service, and in the basement of their house they alternate at the switchboard. Rarely do Mrs. Q. and her daughter leave the house. Mrs. Q., an ugly woman, fat, red-complexioned, with bulging eyes and long, bright orange hair, is suspicious of everything and hates almost everyone. She calls the neighborhood a "black nightmare," where the Negroes have moved in after the Jews. "Robbers and thieves, all of them," she cries. Capote says she is afraid of the changes taking place because she is a woman of attitudes but of no ideas.

Her fear leads her to turn her house into a prison of bars, catches, and locks, guarded further by a loud barking dog.

The neighborhood in which he lives is deteriorating. A baroque-looking church captures his attention. It is abandoned, falling apart. Chalked graffiti defaces the door, and animals are inside the church. Capote says, "The church . . . symbolizes some elements of Brooklyn."

At the Cherokee Hotel, where he often eats dinner, many elderly people are residents. Fighting and pettiness are constant elements. The tenants threaten and insult each other. Ironically, the grandest and most cherished guest of the Cherokee steals the hotel's dime-store silverware.

One particularly lovely winter day Capote takes a walk in Brooklyn Heights with a friend. It is one of the few places he knows that contains the past for him, but it will soon be gone, to give way for highways and a tunnel. The palisades are being destroyed, the old mansions demolished. Towards dusk as the two friends look out across the river at the lights beginning to appear in Manhattan Capote speculates about the city's future ruins. As for Brooklyn, he is convinced it will always be unfathomable. Nobody will ever understand it.

Again, the photographs with the sketch amplify the meaning. The first is a picture of an old, narrow, shabby Victorian house. The garden is unkempt, the trees raggedy. The second photograph shows a small child standing at one of two lace-curtained windows looking out at blankness. The entire composition suggests emptiness and nothingness, which mirror the mood in Capote's prose.

In the sketch, "Hollywood," Capote defines the approach by air to Los Angeles as what he imagines crossing the surface of the moon would be like—lifeless. The scenes shown in the fabled city capture that element of lifelessness or unreality.

He takes a long walk in order to buy some exquisite fruit that he has seen displayed in front of a store, but on touching it discovers it is plastic. The actual fruit that he can purchase from inside the shop is small and not very tasty. Another time, Christmas week, Capote takes a bus ride from Beverly Hills to downtown Los Angeles. Everything he passes along the way is artificial: the motorized sleigh that drops white cornflakes, prefabricated trees, carols sounding through loudspeakers, tinsel in brilliant sun. He finds the holiday out of place in Hollywood, especially since there are so few children.

Yet Hollywood is the mecca which draws many kinds of pilgrims. On the plane he meets a young girl who is headed for Hollywood because the cards have said a job awaits her as a secretary to a movie actress. She has neither plans nor arrangements, and the taxi driver lets her out in the "middle" of the city, on Wilshire Boulevard.[2]

One afternoon the writer and a friend are invited to lunch at the home of a "fabled" actress, a "Miss C." A guard stands at the gate of the estate. Inside the house, as they wait for Miss C. to make her appearance, her daughter entertains them by reciting the cost of various objects in the room. When the actress comes in she is dressed in a flannel robe and wears no makeup. Making her apologies for being late, she informs them that she has been upstairs making beds. Capote lets the irony speak for itself.

At the home of another famous actress the writer is taken into the garden to meet the woman's father, an elderly man. Capote speaks of the love old people have for California. To them "it is a preview of heaven," he says. The old man gives each of the visitors a bracelet made of bottle caps, and speaking in a frail voice that can hardly be heard "through the honeyed blowing air," says, "A merry Christmas, children."

Capote's tones suggest a land of lotus-eaters, a place where it is always afternoon, a land of death. Nothing seems alive, a theme introduced at the beginning of the essay when he describes the sensation of lifelessness in the approach of the plane at Los Angeles.

The photograph that concludes the piece is a harshly mutilated advertisement for a movie. A woman's face is hidden in shadows, her eyes torn away. The writer's choice of pictures underscores the concept of darkness behind the artificial light of an unreal world.

In the sketch "Haiti" the introductory photograph is more like a painting than a picture. Faceless figures appear to be in motion, and there is a great variation of shading, greys, whites, and blacks, making a pastiche effect that also exists in the essay.

A character is introduced to the reader. He is Hyppolite, a successful Haitian primitive painter. He has been married many times and has a number of children. Now a baby daughter has died. Capote muses about the mourning rituals in Haiti.

The author spends his mornings reading on a terrace from which he can look at the mountains and the sea. Although he thinks Haiti is the most interesting part of the West Indies, few tourists come there. Nevertheless, he agrees that the island lacks the attractions visitors might want. The closest beach is several hours away, the restaurants are mediocre, there is little night life.

When Capote describes the life of the prostitutes, the reader is reminded of his story "A House of Flowers." The whore houses are respectable, and the ladies sit on the front porches fanning themselves and drinking beer. One popular lady of the evening saves her money so that one day she can fulfill her ambition of owning a mouthful of gold teeth.[3]

Another link to "A House of Flowers" is introduced when Capote tells a story he has heard from a friend. He saw a girl bound to the trunk of a tree. When a kind old man offered her a drink of water she accepted and then spit the last of the water in the old man's face.

The government is concerned with the impression Haitians make on tourists because the people are so very poor. However, Capote writes, there is a generosity of spirit in the Haitians that is not generally associated with poverty. Impoverished as they are they always bring small gifts to people when they visit.

Haiti is an island given to celebration. When there is to be a carnival, previews are held. Drums are sounded from noon to dusk; groups of people go through the streets singing and dancing, each led by a man in a sparkling suit with feathers in his hair.

During the carnival Capote is taken to a ceremony held by a *houngan,* a Voodoo priest. The temple is a shed that has altar rooms on both sides. Drummers beat a chant that a group of white-clad girls sing as they move around the floor. When the sound of the drums changes, the *houngan* enters. He is very young, yet appears "unaccountably old, asleep, transfixed." Dressed in red silk robes, he gives the impression of birdlike lightness. With corn meal and ashes he draws a *verver,* a design on the ground. Each detail is intricate in the surrealistic pattern, each filled with meaning, as the priest creates a "ferocious web of crowns, criss-crosses, snakes, phallic shapes, eyes, fishtails. The *houngan* returns to the altar room, then reappears dressed in green, carrying a large iron ball. As it catches fire he continues to hold it until it cools, but his hands are not burned. He seems to be caught in a mystical state as his body trembles and his eyes roll

upward into his head. He whirls people across the
verver on the ground. Finally he runs to the unopened
door of the altar, beating upon it until his hands are
bloodied, seeking the "magic: truth's secret, pure
peace." Capote asks whether the priest would have
found the "unobtainable" if the door had ever opened,
and he answers his own question: "That he believed
so is all that matters."

The photo at the end of the essay is of a design
that incorporates many elements, the most provocative
of which are a snake and a heart. The essay itself,
although more interesting in many of its details than
some of the preceding pieces, is less structured. It
rambles more and includes some stories that seem un-
important, even meaningless; one can only assume that
the author believed they added flavor to the whole.

The photograph at the end of the sketch "To
Europe," discloses the essential meaning of the trip
Capote takes with a friend. The picture is that of a
sparkling canal in Venice, with a gondola in the fore-
ground and impressive old buildings across the water.
The voyage is one of delight, even though they meet
some problems along the way.

Capote travels to a number of places, and in
many of them he finds stories among the people he
sees. On a train to Paris he shares the compartment
with several other travelers, among them two elegant
Italian ladies, whose only luggage is a caged parrot.
When the customs officials come aboard they dis-
mantle the cage and find many packages of heroin inside it. The bird, released from its prison, flies out an
open window into the cold night. The ladies are more
concerned with the bird's fate than with their own.

Europe provides the writer with an enormous
sense of pleasure. He feels that all the beauties he has
seen in Europe will be part of him, the gardens, the

flowers of every kind, the music, and the exquisite vistas of mountains and lakes.

In Sirmione, Italy, he stands in the garden of a castle which overlooks Lago di Garda. As he listens to a young man playing a hand harp and watches the swans in the water, he has a sensation of joy, like that of a child hearing a fairy tale. He is filled with the knowledge that his trip to Europe has revived in him a childlike sense of wonder. Only with luck, he notes, can one find a "bridge to childhood." For him it allows a return to the landscape of the imagination.

The introductory photograph also catches the sensation of the marvelous. It shows a plane flying at dusk, but the shape of the plane is distorted so as to suggest a bird with a small body and huge wings. The viewer and reader remember Keats's desire to be carried away on wings of poesy, the same feeling that Capote has as he stands in the magical castle in Sirmione.

In the sketch "Ischia," Capote describes his lengthy stay on the island, which is off the coast of Naples, not far from Capri, the better known and more popular island. He goes there in very early spring, before anything is in bloom, and remains through the intense heat of early summer.

There is a charm about islands, he tells us, which makes people think that only good things can happen. As the author describes his visit to Ischia, that charm seems to hold.

Although most people stay in the capital, Porto, Capote and his friend go to Forio, which is located at the farthest end of the island. After their arrival in Ischia they drive through the evening dusk to their destination. Following the road high above the sea, Capote is able to look at the boats on the water as well as the goats on the hillsides, and the flutter of lamps and candles in the cafés they pass. The island has no electricity, and at his hotel he discovers there is no running water.

There is much poverty on the island. People are without work, but the cost of living is very low. Thus Capote and his friend pay very little for two large rooms overlooking the sea, maid service, and enormous meals complete with wine.

In contrast to the privation of the people is the elaborate jewelry bestowed on the figure of a new statue of the Virgin when it is brought to Ischia. Although her face is covered with a black veil, the rest of her is bedecked with a great number of watches of silver and gold. The arrival of the statue is a momentous event in the life of the islanders, and they decorate their streets and balconies for the parade. Incongruously, a military band plays as the Virgin is carried on a litter through the streets.

Among the poor people Capote meets are some members of the Mussolini family, the widow and three of her children. He finds the "sad and sympathetic" Signora Mussolini as shabby as any other island woman, and she is a person who almost never smiles.

The changing seasons are mirrored in the two photographs that introduce and conclude the piece. The first shows a fisherman mending his net on a dark day. The seascape is rocky. The second picture combines beauty and ugliness: flowers grow up a wall above which laundry hangs.

Many lemon and orange trees grow on the island, and on the mountainsides grapes are grown for the much-praised wine of Ischia. Along the cliffs blossoms grow in abundance, and below, the water of the ocean is so clear that one can see the fish swimming. In the hot summer everything turns into color. Time seems to expand so that the days and nights appear longer. All is quiet in the middle of the day when people take their siestas, but then everything comes to life again. People linger out of doors as long as they can in the brightness and beauty of the season.

"Ischia" has the quality of a painting. Capote captures in it color, line, and tone.

Some of the same pictorial aspect is reflected in the eighth piece in the collection, "Tangier." This section has less form than the preceding piece, however, because it contains a number of little stories about the people who have settled in the region.

Many foreigners love the area and will not leave. There are a great many celebrities among them. Perhaps they are drawn by the marvelous climate, or the exquisite beaches, or the sophisticated night life that goes on until dawn. It is a captivating place that tempts one to stay forever. It is also a fine city to hide in, and Capote notes that there is violence and intrigue everywhere.

One summer evening during the holy season of *Ramadan,* the author and his friend decide to drive to the beach of Sidi Kacem to see the celebration that follows *Ramadan,* the month of abstinence. It is the custom for Arabs from all over Morocco to go to Sidi Kacem at the end of the month. There they create a city of lights and cafés for three days of celebration. Music, dancing, and tea drinking are the activities.

Capote describes the magnificence of the sky, filled with shooting stars. And at sunrise when there is a joyful sound from the people, he is filled with regret that morning brings back his world and time.

Spain is a mixture of harshness and beauty, Capote suggests through his sketch "A Ride through Spain." It is rugged, as shown by the photograph of the Spanish houses built into a rocky hillside. And it is gentle, as revealed in the scene of a castle which, rising amidst flowering trees, seems to belong in a fairy tale. It brings to mind that bridge which allows the author to return to the landscape of the imagination, to which he refers in the piece, "To Europe."

In "A Ride through Spain" Capote is on an old train going from Granada to Algeciras, a seaport looking toward Africa. On the afternoon of the journey the sound of machine guns is heard. Capote calls out, "Bandits," and is immediately echoed in Spanish by the other passengers. They huddle in fright on the floor until a soldier comes seeking a doctor. The people learn that there are no bandits, but that an old man has fallen from the train and injured himself. A soldier had then fired a gun to stop the train.

While the doctor and the soldiers take care of the old man, the passengers stroll happily through the woods. Only one of the passengers does not join in, and she is very scornful of Capote when the group reassembles. As the train starts up again, there is the lovely sight of butterflies at the window. Bandits, guns, and trouble seem remote from the natural scene presented for the reader. The butterflies bring harmony and serenity. Thus *Local Color* concludes.

Capote's next published work of nonfiction was *The Muses Are Heard,* originally written as articles for *The New Yorker*.

In December 1955, a touring American theatrical company went to the Russian cities of Leningrad and Moscow to present the musical show, *Porgy and Bess*. Historically, more than musically, it was an event of some importance, for it represented a new type of cultural exchange program between America and the USSR. The book, *The Muses Are Heard,* is Capote's eye-witness account of the trip.

As one of the three journalists (Capote considers himself a reporter on this occasion) accompanying the group, which consists of a huge cast and their families, as well as other personnel involved in the production, Capote has the opportunity to observe

theater people in unusual circumstance. During the
time it takes to reach their destination and the days
that follow in Leningrad through the opening of the
show, Capote records what he sees and hears. He
re-creates for the reader both the gloom and splen-
dor of Leningrad, the awesome loneliness of its bitter
climate, and a sense of daily life in Russia. With his
finely tuned ear for dialogue as well as his strong in-
stinct for humor, he captures the personalities of the
Americans and Russians he meets.

The title of the book was taken from a Russian
saying that Capote was to hear spoken several times
by an official from the Russian Ministry of Culture.
He and four other Russian delegates who joined the
troupe after their train crossed the Polish-Russian bor-
der remained with them throughout the tour. In greet-
ing the Americans aboard the train the delegate commends their trip as an undertaking for peace and then
makes the statement which is, says Capote, "the starring sentence of all future speeches." The delegate
concludes his welcome with the pronouncement:
"When the cannons are heard, the muses are silent;
when the cannons are silent, the muses are heard."

Although the tour was intended to serve the cause
of goodwill, it was not financed by the American State
Department, which had previously sponsored *Porgy
and Bess* for several years in a number of foreign
countries. The reason for the Department's "disinherit-
ing" but "not disowning" was never clear. What
spokesmen said was that the trip proposed by the
producers was "politically premature." When monetary support was denied by the State Department, the
Russians capitalized the venture. As it turned out,
the Russians were the financial beneficiaries and the
company lost money: their weekly fee was reduced,
and half of it was paid in Russian rubles whose value
was considerably less than American dollars.

Capote speculates that the material of *Porgy and Bess* had to be a matter of concern to both American and Russian diplomats. Russia, which is both puritanical and atheistic, would be shocked by the overt sexuality of the production and hostile to the religious message; furthermore, a country which prides itself on rationality would object to the support of superstition; and finally, says Capote humorously, the Russians would certainly not be happy with an opera whose theme is "people can be happy with plenty of nothin'."

Then why would the Russians permit the tour of *Porgy and Bess*? Because it serves the purpose of propaganda, he reasons. The basic story concerns poor blacks and exploitive whites, a perfect target for Soviet criticism. As it turned out, however, propagandistic statements after opening night "seemed a mere pianissimo compared" to what some people had expected.

Capote's story of the experiences of the group at many points is pure satire. For the most part he avoids personal commentary, allowing dialogue and events to provide the humor. Characteristic is an early briefing in Berlin by officials from the American Embassy in Moscow; warning the company about the Soviet system, the consul says that though the Russians are "nice," their government is "bad," and that the troupe must remember that it is hostile to ours. Capote captures the simplistic nature of the session by quoting such statements, and describing the speaker's "slow, spelling-it-out tones." But the author does not confine his efforts only to American officialdom. He does as much for the Russians. He also satirizes one of the producers of *Porgy and Bess*, Robert Breen, as a man of dual personality, someone who rehearses "impromptu" curtain calls; Mrs. Breen, in her single-minded devotion to her husband, a woman of "immaculate enthusiasm"; Warner Watson, a production assistant, whose ambition in the undertaking is to get everything "fenced in"; and Lee Gershwin, wife of Ira, coauthor of the opera. Mrs. Gershwin, a diamond-studded woman, sees everything in terms of endearment, so that the Russian system of surveillance is "darling," making one "feel so protected." Members of the cast and their idiosyncrasies provide opportunities for comedy, as do Capote's fellow journalists, particularly Leonard Lyons of the *New York Post* newspaper.

The woman delegate of the Russian Ministry of Culture provides an irresistible target for Capote's humor. In Miss Lydia he sketches a memorable comic character, a mixture of seriousness and good cheer. She is extraordinarily simple. With ideas both limited and naive, she is unable to understand any subtlety. In contrast to the Americans she is dowdy and unsophisticated. When a heavy, unappealing, almost inedible meal is served aboard the train headed for Leningrad, Miss Lydia eats everything in sight, urging the others to do likewise. With unconscious humor she gives the highest praise to the meal, unaware that her American dinner companions have been hungrily looking forward to caviar with blini and vodka. Unwittingly, she completely ruins their hopes, saying "You will not obtain better in Moscow itself."

Miss Lydia's genial translations and flowery English present a strong contrast to the trim, grey, sunless landscape through which the train travels on its way from East Berlin to Warsaw to Brest-Litovsk to Leningrad. Going to sleep on the overcrowded, dirty, uncomfortable train, she proclaims it is time "to dream," to go to "unravel the sleeve of care." After arrival in Leningrad, there is a great deal of confusion about the hotel rooms, but Miss Lydia tries to soothe everyone. There are plenty of hotel rooms, she announces, and "no one will stride the streets."

The hotel, its employees, the Institut De Beauté

—an elegant name for a dreary hairdressing salon—cafés, shopping, all are described by the writer for comic effect. Buying an expensive fur hat that turns out not to fit and also to be fake takes Capote a long time in a store. The system is needlessly complex, made more so by a clerk's figuring the cost on an abacus. "An efficient method no doubt," says Capote mockingly, "still, some clever Soviet should invent the cash register."

All, however, is not funny. In brief but detailed episodes the writer communicates his sense of the sinister in Russian life. One late afternoon he walks around St. Isaac's Cathedral. "Night swept the sky like the black crows that wheeled and cawed overhead." And always the bitter cold. Then he sees four men quietly and brutally beating a man near the wall of the church. A woman stands nearby calmly waiting. Soon the Russian whom Capote has arranged to meet drives up in a taxi and pulls him into the car furiously, telling him he is an idiot, that one should avoid situations of that kind.

Later, in a workmen's café, a young musician tries to enlist Capote's help. The boy, whose father was English, wants Capote to write to the British ambassador so that he can go to England. But Capote cannot help him. Looking at the young man he sees despair in the wet eyes, and an expression which reminds him of the man beaten and left on the sidewalk next to the cathedral.

Hopelessness or gloom is everywhere. In the cafés to which Capote is taken, patrons consume vast quantities of alcohol; yet there seems to be little pleasure. People are afraid to talk. Secrecy and fear are part of the atmosphere. Even the music in the hotel night-club is lackluster. Only when some American musicians from the company take over the bandstand is the place enlivened. Then briefly the crowd is "transfigured." Russians, who have been sitting in boredom ignoring the Russian band, immediately are caught up by the American jazz. They smile, tap their feet, crowd the bandstand, and fill the dance floor.

The spontaneous reaction to the jazz differs considerably from that of the Russian audience to the premiere of *Porgy and Bess*. The audience, which doesn't understand the language or the story, is also foreign to "the music, the style of dancing, the directorial approach." The sexual daring shocks them, and the most famous songs go unapplauded. By the end of the first act many of the American observers are concerned that the show is a failure. But the second act, more comprehensible to the Russians, improves the atmosphere. "And," says Capote, "though the performance did not sail, perhaps because too much water had already been shipped, at least it floated, wallowed along in a current of less than frigid temperature."

As he leaves the theater, Capote hears some of the audience humming or singing bits and pieces from the show. He remembers that a Russian acquaintance told him earlier that when summer comes one would be able to walk near the river and hear the sounds of *Porgy and Bess* being whistled. When the reviews come out, both the Russian and the American notices are good. Still, Capote does not really know how to evaluate the opening of the opera. He decides that it has been a success of sorts, one whose long-range effect would be significant.

Everyone in the company is delighted with the congratulatory cables sent from home. When one member of the cast says happily that they have made history, Watson, the production assistant of the company, asserts, "we've got *history* fenced in."

Although few people would argue the significance of a cultural breakthrough in the cold war between the United States and the Soviet Union, it is not likely

that many people remember the tour of the company
of *Porgy and Bess*. For something as ephemeral as
performance, the event must be fixed by some more
lasting means: a tape, a film, or a book. Thus it is the
writer who has actually "fenced in" history. Capote, in
recording the trip of the American company, has
also caught the essence of life in Russia, and that in
itself is timeless.

The Muses Are Heard, like *Local Color*, was
republished in 1973 in the collection *The Dogs Bark*,
which contains a large and varied number of essays.
There is the piece entitled "Jane Bowles," which was
the introduction to *The Collected Work of Jane
Bowles*,[4] and another, "Cecil Beaton," which was the
preface to *The Best of Beaton*. Reprinted also in
The Dogs Bark, as well as in the earlier *Selected Writings* (1963), is one of Capote's best-known journalistic
pieces. Entitled "The Duke in His Domain," it is part
interview with Marlon Brando and part narrative
about him.

During the filming of a James Michener novel,
Sayonara, in 1957, Capote met with Brando in Kyoto,
to do a portrait of the actor for *The New Yorker* magazine. The two had become acquainted years before,
when Capote attended a rehearsal of *A Streetcar
Named Desire*, and some of what the writer has to say
is a comparison of the young Brando with the now
famous actor. He delineates the force of Brando's individuality, at least as he seemed to Capote the night
of the interview, for Brando never means all that he
states, and his parting remarks are, "Don't pay too
much attention to what I say. I don't always feel the
same way."

The Brando Capote describes has a reputation
among his colleagues of the Sayonara company as
friendly, yet remote. In spite of his general helpfulness
and amiability, he doesn't socialize with the rest of the

crew. Even on the set, when he isn't working he reads philosophy and writes frequently in a notebook. Brando never reads fiction, yet he wants to write it, a clue to the complex character of the man.

Capote goes to Brando's suite at the hotel for dinner. Brando's appetites reflect a dichotomy of the near teetotaler and the glutton, a paradoxical man; Capote remembers their first meeting, when he was impressed by Brando's appearance, the strong athletic body and the refined poetic head. Brando has always been able to change himself for the requirements of the role. The character Stanley Kowalski in Tennessee Williams's play, which made Brando a star, differs completely from the sensitive, searching actor who worries about prejudice, friendship, and love.

Speaking of friendship to Capote, Brando asserts that many of his friends are misfits in society, but he offers them himself as a center, a focus for their attention. He characterizes himself in terms that Capote finds significant enough to use for his title: "I'm the duke. Sort of the duke of my domain."

Brando has a great need for affection. Perhaps, Capote suggests, it is the result of childhood unhappiness, an indifferent father, a mother who drank. Caring intensely for his mother, Brando tried to help her when he left the Midwest and went to New York to work. His mother lived with him for awhile, but it was of no use. The mother "broke apart like a piece of porcelain," and Brando gave up his attempt to save her. As he tells Capote about it, he is like a hurt, sad child.

There is also in Brando a streak of the ascetic. He longs for more than the success of stardom. He wants his fame to have substance or else it is without meaning, like "sitting on a pile of candy." Glory is not enough. Fearing a life that will not go anywhere, he tells Capote he is going to simplify it in the future.

But whatever he does, he must have a fence around his home in order to protect himself from writers.

The fence, the gluttony, the painful revelations are all part of the exceedingly complex man Capote has met. As the writer walks back to his hotel in the early morning hours, through the quiet Kyoto streets, he sees a huge advertisement for a popular Brando film. The actor is shown in a seated position, smiling serenely. Capote, looking at the poster, summarizes his responses to Brando: godlike, but also a person atop "a pile of candy."

In this depiction of Brando, Capote is supremely skillful, never intruding himself, always focusing on the subject, a technique that was to be central in the reporting for *In Cold Blood*. In "The Duke in His Domain," the pen of the creative novelist is also at work, as Capote captures the foreign flavor of the city in its beauty and mystery. The city, like the actor, is a paradoxical mixture; and both are unknowable.

In 1959, Richard Avedon and Truman Capote combined forces to create *Observations,* a book of portraits and commentary. Predictably, the work has become a collector's item because of its series of stunning photographs. The accompanying prose portraits are in Capote's reportorial style, that is, a mixture of journalism and creative prose. Avedon captures "a moment focused by his perception," as well as the essence of the sitter's personality. But Capote ranges further than the moment; he also tells the reader of the way the great and famous achieved their renown. In anecdotes and images he adds color to the black, grey, and white of the photographs.

Appropriately, Capote speaks first of Avedon, a somewhat inarticulate man whose voice is heard through his work.

Avedon started taking pictures with a box camera

when he was a ten-year-old; precocious, unhappy, unable to get along with his father who despaired of his son's lack of interest in education, he left home early to join the Merchant Marine instead of finishing high school. In the service he gained some formal training in photography. Later, he went on to study at the New York School for Social Research. Because he took a course taught by the art director of *Harper's Bazaar*, he established the connections vital to the launching of his career. Summarizing Avedon's success, Capote asserts that his work was new and fresh, that he had a combination of talent and "staying power," which made him "aesthetically influential."

Finding more beauty in older people than in the young, Avedon chose subjects who are "obsessed with work of one sort or another." The photographs that appear in the book were selected from those taken during a fifteen-year period.

From the film industry there are movie stars Charlie Chaplin, Humphrey Bogart, Mae West, and Marilyn Monroe, as well as the Italian screen writer Cesare Zavattini, and the American film director John Huston; two famed artists are included, the Spanish Picasso and the French Duchamp; there are portraits from the musical world, of Louis Armstrong, who is part of the history of American jazz, and of dancers, one flamenco, Escudero, and one Russian Bolshoi ballerina, Maya Plisetskaya; also from the world of entertainment is French circus star Emilien Bouglione; society beauties, or "swans" as Capote labels them, are shown: Madame Agnelli and Mrs. William (Babe) Paley, for many years one of Capote's dearest friends. And there is a French hostess, Marie-Louise Bousquet, and a world-famous designer, Coco Chanel. Writers of various kinds comprise the largest number of sitters: two American poets, Marianne Moore and Ezra Pound;

The New Yorker reporter in Paris, Genêt—Janet Flan-
ner. Among the writers there are six novelists: two
from the American South, Carson McCullers and Eu-
dora Welty; the English writer, Somerset Maugham;
the Danish Baroness Blixen, who took the pseudonym
Isak Dinesen; the French novelists André Gide and
Jean Cocteau, the latter also identified by Capote as
"poet . . . playwright, journalist, designer, painter, inventor of ballets, film-maker, professional conversa-
tionalist." Completing the list of subjects are the
French diver, Cousteau; two Englishmen, a priest, Father Darcy, and a photographer, Cecil Beaton; American physicist J. Robert Oppenheimer; and finally, the
designer of the book, *Observations,* and Avedon's early
teacher, Alexey Brodovitch.

Without the photographs only a limited number
of the commentaries are meaningful for the purposes
of abstraction.[5] Capote chose the seven most acces-
sible ones for the collection *The Dogs Bark.* Those
do not require the camera's eye to speak to the reader.

In the essay "Isak Dinesen," Capote describes a
visit with the celebrated writer of Gothic tales. He
goes to Rungsted, a village located "between Copen-
hagen and Elsinore," to meet the frail, old "legend,"
Baroness Blixen. A woman who has led an adventure-
filled life, the Baroness lived and worked in Africa for
a long time, and when she lost her home there, returned to Denmark. During the Second World War
her "house was a way station for Jews escaping to
Sweden. Jews in the kitchen and Nazis in the garden,"
she tells Capote. But she makes little of her bravery.

Capote speaks of both Dinesen's extraordinary
presence and also her affirmation of life. Because there
are frequent references to infirmity and great age,
the reader knows as Capote does that the Baroness is
close to death; yet, at the end, the impression left is of

timelessness, not only in Dinesen's acceptance of all that life brings but also in the truth and beauty of her art.

"Mae West" depicts another legendary figure. In the essay Capote tells a story to reveal the dichotomy between public perception of the actress and the lady herself. A tea party was given in New York for Miss West, who was performing in a nightclub show. The honored guest was hours late in arriving, and when she did her personality bore no resemblance to what people expected. Although her appearance was a replica of that on the screen—brassy hair, endless eyelashes, pale skin, and a body that was the "Big Ben of hourglass figures," she was not the sexy siren her publicity proclaimed. She was nervous, shy, and defenseless. In unfamiliar surroundings, Miss West found it difficult, if not impossible, to talk with the men and women at the party.

The brief sketch "Louis Armstrong" tells more about Capote than about the musician. Capote first met "The Satch" in 1928, when he was four years old. All summer long he traveled back and forth by steamer between New Orleans and St. Louis. Armstrong was kind and generous to the little boy, telling him he was talented and belonged in vaudeville. At night when he was entertaining the crowd, the trumpet player would call on the child "to do a little tap dance," and afterwards Capote would pass around the straw hat that Armstrong had given him. When summer ended, however, so did the boy's career. Some years later, when he was ten, lonely and unhappy in a boarding school, he wrote to the musician asking if he could get him a job in a nightclub. Armstrong didn't answer, but even so, writes Capote, "I still loved him, still do."

In 1950, when Capote was living in Taormina,

Sicily, he met André Gide, who was then a very old man.[6] The essay, "Jean Cocteau and André Gide," tells of the relationship between the two Frenchmen, and of the differences in their writings. Capote judges Gide's work as sincere but without imagination, and Cocteau's as the reverse, reflecting his character as well, "vaguely imaginative but vivaciously insincere." Throughout their lives Gide has always felt uncomfortable in Cocteau's presence. When Cocteau arrives in Taormina, Capote calls him a "rainbow-winged and dancing dragonfly" and Gide "the toad." Cocteau is a man of the twentieth century, and that, states Capote, is the source of Gide's dislike, for the old writer wants to be more than a man of his time. Although Capote thinks that an admirable wish, his preference is clearly for Cocteau, and he asks if it is not "possible that a man who has so enlivened our today will, if not overflow, at least trickle into somebody's tomorrow?"

Bogart, Capote says in the verbal portrait of "Humphrey Bogart," used two words which were keys to understanding him: "bum" and "professional." Some of Bogart's bums, among others, were people who didn't provide for their families, men who cheated sexually or financially. The professional was the man who did his job right, the man of discipline. It was the discipline of doing perfectly what he had to do, Capote says, that kept Bogart's art alive after he was gone.

In the sketch "Ezra Pound," Capote paints with broad strokes the life of the poet from the day of his birth in 1885, in Idaho, to his release from a hospital for the insane in 1958, when he was seventy-two. Pound's face is represented as a "satyr-saint's," and that kind of split in his temperament marked all of his life. The man who was so generous that he spent much of his early life helping friends artistically and financially was also a destroyer. In the thirties and forties he became a devotee of Italian fascism. Radio broadcasts that he made from Italy during World War II led to his eventual indictment and imprisonment. During the twelve years he was kept in St. Elizabeth's Hospital he wrote the *Pisan Cantos,* for which he was awarded the Bollingen Prize.

Capote's sympathies are with Pound, suggesting that he was no more insane than any other poet, and attacking those who carped about the poetry award to Pound. One feels Capote's pity for the poet as he speaks of him as a man forever entrapped.

"Marilyn Monroe," the last of the selections from *Observations* to appear in *The Dogs Bark,* makes some of the points that have become familiar in the two decades since the suicide of the actress. A reader of the sketch is impressed by the fact that Capote saw in Monroe the anxiety, pathos, and insecurity that brought about her death only a few years after *Observations* was published.

Capote compares the actress to an ice-cream concoction, "untidy but divine"; her lips, her hair, her body have made her famous. Off the screen few people recognize her. Yet the impression she gives on film and the one she presents in person are the same, that of "a waif-figure." Monroe "is an orphan, in spirit and actually." This, says Capote, has two opposing sides, for although Monroe has little confidence in people, she works very hard at winning them over. And she succeeds. People feel sorry for her at the same time they are dazzled by her.

Noting that Monroe's husband, Arthur Miller, has referred to her as an "institution" and a "symbol," Capote decries the use of such gloomy terms to describe the actress. However, at this point his essay fizzles out, as it ends in an arch description of Monroe.

When Capote published *The Dogs Bark* he included in it four travel-type essays written between 1951 and 1959: "Fontana Vecchia," 1951; "Lola," 1964;

"A House on the Heights," 1959; "Greek Paragraphs," 1968.[7] The style and the subject matter of the four selections resemble those in *Local Color*.

In "Fontana Vecchia" Capote describes life in Taormina, Sicily. He and a friend leased an ancient house high in the mountains outside of town. Life in that part of Italy is very primitive, although Taormina was once a popular resort. The only worthwhile foods are fish and pasta; meat and poultry are so scarce that his cook does not know how to prepare a chicken.

The seasons shape the life of the peasants. For the few visitors who still come to the town there is very little to do except shop or dawdle over a drink. But he enjoys the benefits of the former tourist area and is pleased there are no tourists. In good weather there are the beaches, most of them deserted. Capote discovers the joy of snorkeling, with all the colors of underwater life. As the essay concludes, winter is settling in, but he is content.

"Lola" is the name of a raven a young Italian girl gives Capote as a Christmas present. Although Capote dislikes the bird intensely at first, he soon becomes attached to her. Because the bird's wings have been clipped she does not fly. Capote tries to teach her how, but it is to no avail.

When trouble besets the servant girl she blames it on the raven, who, she claims, is taking vengeance on her for having cut its wings. Villagers soon become convinced that Capote's house and the writer himself have the evil eye. As a result he leaves Sicily and goes to Rome, taking the bird with him.

In Rome Capote rents a penthouse with a balcony where the raven likes to sit. One day Lola is frightened by a cat and she falls from the balcony onto a passing truck. Trying to catch up with the vehicle Capote runs down stairs, falls, breaks his glasses, but he is too late; the bird is gone.

"A House on the Heights" is an essay in praise of one part of Brooklyn. The writer delights in the view across the river, and the elegant old houses, and relishes the idea that famed authors have lived in the section.

He moves to a beautiful, old yellow house on Willow Street, where he becomes friendly with some of the neighborhood people. The restaurants suit him and he talks of the delicasies they serve. Strolling along the river road or across the bridge is another of his enthusiasms, pleasurable in any season. However, one night as he walks through a poor neighborhood he is harassed by a gang called the "Cobras." Fortunately, a storm comes up, and he makes it safely back to his yellow house.

In "Greek Paragraphs" Capote tells of a cruise he took through the Greek Islands. The only passenger on the yacht because of a death in the family of his host, Capote sails off with the crew from Piraeus to a number of other islands, ending the voyage in Rhodes. During the trip he keeps notes describing fruits and wines, starlight, music, and weather. He also repeats a gruesome tale the captain tells him of a young crippled English boy torn to pieces and eaten by rats on a remote Greek island. At another point the writer describes a house on the beach at Lindos that he is tempted to buy. Although the house is both beautiful and cheap, he decides against it because of "politics, old mortality, inconvenient emotional attachments, the impossibilities of the Greek tongue," but he knows he is making a mistake. Later, in the heat and dust of Athens he remembers "the stone house in the blue cove."

In each of the four essays—as in the collection in *Local Color*—Capote creates a sense of place. Each landscape is delineated with its unique quality. The remoteness and silence of Taormina is different from the quiet river walks of Brooklyn. Even violence in America has another essence from that of Italy. The Cobras who challenge Capote bear no resemblance to the harsh Italian peasants who beat their women.

Capote is like a painter in these sketches. He brushes in color upon color, shading, adding tonal quality. These are more than travel pieces or journalistic reports or anecdotes. They are all of these; in reading them along with the other essays and portraits of this period one may see the techniques that were vital to the writing of *In Cold Blood*.

8

Acts of Darkness:
In Cold Blood

One morning in November, 1959, as Capote was looking through the *New York Times,* a headline caught
his eye: "Wealthy Farmer, 3 of Family Slain." The
report which followed stated briefly that Herbert
Clutter, a wheat and cattle farmer, his wife, and their
teenaged son and daughter had been killed in their
home in Holcomb, a suburb of Garden City, Kansas.
Soon after reading the account, Capote decided that
the story of the crime was what he had been searching
for, a subject that would enable him to write a book
which would endure; further, he was tempted by the
thought of an area and people that were unfamiliar to
him.

    After making arrangements to do a series on the
Clutter murders for *The New Yorker* magazine,
Capote turned to his Random House publisher,
Bennett Cerf, for help in meeting people in Kansas,
a state he'd never visited. Cerf phoned a friend, Dr.
James McCain, president of Kansas State University,
who promised letters of introduction "to half the
people in Kansas," [1] in exchange for Capote's meeting
one evening with the members of the English Department. A few days after he had read the story, Capote
was on his way to Kansas with his childhood friend,
Harper Lee. Lee stayed with Capote about two
months, helping in a variety of ways—getting to know

people who would be useful to Capote, going on interviews with him, and keeping notes that he could refer to when necessary. Not only did Capote meet the principals in the case but also large numbers of townspeople, some of whom became his friends.

Five and a half years after the Clutter murders, the case came to an end with the execution of the criminals, Richard Eugene Hickock and Perry Edward Smith. Capote's book about the crime appeared shortly afterwards, in January, 1966, a literary sensation critically and commercially. A work that sold fifty thousand copies a week within the first four months of publication, *In Cold Blood* remained on the best-seller list for more than a year, one of the great financial successes in publishing history. The book was translated into twenty-five foreign languages and was made into a popular and highly regarded film.

In earlier years Capote had trained himself not to write or use a tape recorder during interviews, but instead to make notes from memory afterwards, a technique that provoked criticism from various reviewers when *In Cold Blood* was published. Some were never satisfied about the authenticity of the information and took the time to retrace all of Capote's steps to check the facts. There were, however, many more defenders than detractors, and the subject provided a long and lively debate amongst the critics.

After his first reading about the case, Capote spent considerable time preparing to write about it. In addition to investigating intensively the lives of both the victims and the killers, he also did much research on crime. Besides interviewing Hickock and Smith, Capote met with a number of other murderers to gain understanding of what he considers the criminal mentality. When he began the book he had accumulated six thousand pages of notes. By the time it was completed, he had in his possession a huge collection of files containing research material, letters, newspaper clippings, court records, and the belongings of Perry Smith (his books, letters, paintings, and drawings).

Capote defines *In Cold Blood* as an innovative art form, to which he has given the name "nonfiction novel." Combining journalism with the techniques of fiction, the work as Capote describes it is imaginative narrative reporting, new both to journalism and to fiction. An experienced and talented reporter, as evidenced by his essays and nonfiction books, Capote believes himself to be a rare example of the creative writer who has taken journalism seriously. Capote's claim, however, to have developed a unique art form has been another source of controversy among literary critics, and the field has been split by those who see his work as documentary, as fiction, or as art—that is, creative journalism.

Not only are the theme and characters intriguing, but so also are the methods Capote used to establish the reality of the drama he unfolds. Mingling realism with novelistic imagination, Capote gives the facts, disclosing them not in straightforward newspaper fashion but as a creative artist selecting details, positioning them, and reiterating them much as a painter repeats a line or color for meaning or intensity. The structural pattern also suggests film technique with its use of flashback and close-ups, its carefully depicted settings, the gathering momentum behind the escape, pursuit, and capture of the criminals, the crowd scenes, and the courtroom episodes. The tension of the narrative increases as the hunters—the murderers—become the hunted, and as they, the victimizers of a small innocent family, become (according to Capote's presentation) the victims of the large bureaucratic system of criminal justice in Kansas.

The story of the murder of an exemplary American family, an act of apparently "motiveless malig-

nity," [2] carries a universal appeal for readers, no matter how they view its ultimate meaning: as symbol
of violence in America; as the failure of the American Dream; or as a social study of death-obsessed
criminals.

The book is divided into four titled sections of
equal length, each part containing a number of vignettes. Some of these little stories are extremely brief;
one is a single paragraph of nine sentences. The longest segment in the work provides significant information about Perry Smith, the man who interested
Capote more than anyone else in the case.

Structurally the work is designed to provide max-
imum suspense, a masterful accomplishment, inasmuch as newspaper reports had given the reader
knowledge of the outcome. Capote moves back and
forth, first between the criminals and the victims and
then between the detectives and the criminals, creating
the effect of a montage: we see Smith and Hickock
relentlessly moving toward the Clutters as they live
out the final day of their lives; after the crime, the
quiet, careful investigation and pursuit are put into
motion as Smith and Hickock take to the road, imag-
ining themselves home-free, believing they have escaped without leaving a clue behind.

Capote adds to the forcefulness of the story,
particularly in the first section, by establishing an
atmosphere of fatality about the unsuspecting Clutter
family. Mr. Clutter walks through his much loved or-
chard of fruit trees alongside the river, "unaware it
would be his last" day. Nancy, his daughter, hours before her death readies her clothes for church the next
morning, clothing in which she would later be buried.
Each little picture of the Clutters contains an element
of doom. A bookmark inside the Bible on Mrs. Clutter's night table reads: "Take ye heed, watch and
pray: for ye know not when the time is."

In contrast to the unseen and hidden darkness gathering around the victims, in Part I of the book Smith and Hickock seem to have a cloudless sky. No shadow hangs over them as they prepare for the long journey that will end with their own deaths: "Scrubbed, combed, as tidy as two dudes setting off on a double date," they set out to make their "score."

"The Last to See Them Alive," the first part of the work, begins with a description of Holcomb, a village in the wheat plains of western Kansas. A small, shabby-looking town, belying the prosperity of the farm ranchers of Finney County, Holcomb had few attractions for outsiders. Not even the Santa Fe train stopped there. But it was that area to which two former convicts were drawn, to a Holcomb farm some miles from the center of town, which was a small community of Garden City, the county seat.

River Valley Farm was owned by the rich and prominent rancher Herbert Clutter, well known not only in the Midwest but also in Washington, where he had served on the Federal Farm Credit Board in the administration of President Eisenhower. At the farm, an attractive, two-story, fourteen-room, white frame and brick house, Mr. Clutter lived with his wife, Bonnie, their sixteen-year-old daughter, Nancy, and their son, Kenyon, aged fifteen. Two other daughters lived elsewhere: in Illinois, Eveanna, the eldest, a married woman with a young son; in Kansas City, Beverly, a nursing student, engaged to be married Christmas week.

The Clutter farm was a large one on which Herbert Clutter grew numerous crops and raised many cattle. There were also animals that belonged to the children, among which was a favorite, an old horse named Babe that Nancy loved to ride around the farm. One resident employee, Alfred Stoecklein, worked on the farm. He, his wife, and their three children, the only nearby neighbors of the Clutters, had a house less than a hundred yards from them. Yet on the night of the murders, the Stoeckleins heard nothing from the main house. Another regular employee, a day worker, was the housekeeper, Mrs. Helm, whose husband, Paul, worked for the Clutters as a hired man. The Helms did not live on the Clutter property, but both were observant people who were able to provide the detectives with useful background information.

The day of the crime was a beautiful Saturday in November. Mr. Clutter rose later than usual that Indian Summer morning, because the night before the family had gone to see Nancy play Becky Thatcher in a school production of *Tom Sawyer*. Mrs. Clutter, a nervous woman with long-standing psychiatric problems, always slept late, sometimes spending the entire day in bed. Nancy and her boyfriend, Bobby Rupp, had been out past midnight, an occurrence that upset Mr. Clutter, but he was more concerned with the longtime romance between Nancy and Bobby because of the religious differences of the families. He wanted Nancy to sever the relationship, for the Rupps were Roman Catholics and the Clutters, Methodists. In the Bible Belt tradition and as a church leader, Mr. Clutter would never approve of a marriage between his daughter and Bobby. This division and the notation in Nancy's diary that Bobby had visited late Saturday night made Bobby a prime suspect in the case for a short period of time.

Nancy, a clever, highly organized girl, had every moment of that Saturday scheduled: helping one neighborhood child, Jolene, make a cherry pie, rehearsing another youngster with a trumpet solo, running errands for her mother, sewing bridesmaids' dresses for her sister's wedding, making lunch for the family, and taking her horse Babe for her Saturday jaunt to the river.

While Nancy was teaching Jolene to bake, her father was in his office buying a forty-thousand-dollar life insurance policy which paid double indemnity in the case of accidental death. Mr. Clutter made his first payment with a check because he "was famous for never carrying cash." After the murders the check was still in the salesman's pocket. Not only was there double indemnity but also double irony: the irony of Clutter's buying life insurance the day of his death, and the irony of being chosen by Dick Hickock for a robbery, Clutter being a man who never kept any cash on hand.

Mrs. Clutter, after visiting briefly with Jolene in the kitchen, returned to her bed for the remainder of the day. Her husband and son went to a 4-H club meeting, and after they returned Kenyon worked on a hope chest he was making for his engaged sister. Later in the day he went out of doors, where Mr. Helm was working on Mrs. Clutter's garden. As the afternoon turned to dusk, Nancy rode across the field from the river. The three chatted for a time, and as Mr. Helm left for his own house he looked back once. It "was the last I seen them," he said. "Nancy leading old Babe off to the barn."

However, the last friend to see Nancy and Kenyon as well as Herb Clutter was Bobby Rupp, who spent the evening watching television with them. When Bobby got ready to leave, Nancy walked outside with him and the two made a date to go to the movies the following night. But by then Nancy was dead.

While the Clutter family went about their usual routine, hundreds of miles away two young men began their relentless journey toward River Valley Farm.

Perry Smith and Dick Hickock had shared a cell in Kansas State Penitentiary, both imprisoned on charges of theft. Four months after his parole, Perry returned to Kansas, although one condition of his release was that he stay out of that state. Nevertheless, when Dick wrote him about the possibility of a "score," Perry agreed to meet him in Olathe, a suburb of Kansas City, four hundred miles from the Holcomb area, where they would carry out Dick's plan. In actuality, Perry was hoping to find another person, someone he called his "real and only friend," a petty thief by the name of Willie-Jay.[3] Perry's friend had been the chaplain's clerk in prison and had tried to interest Perry in religion. Perry was flattered by Willie-Jay's admiration of his abilities as artist and poet and also by the attention Willie-Jay paid to his psychological and emotional state. Knowing that his friend was due to be released from prison, Perry hoped to find him at the bus terminal in Kansas City. But Willie-Jay left before Perry arrived. Having nothing and nobody to deter him, Perry became committed to Dick's plan.

Dick had decided while he was in prison that Perry would be a useful accomplice in a crime. He believed Perry to be a murderer, because Perry had boasted of once killing a black man. In fact, Perry had invented the story.

Both men agree when planning the robbery at River Valley that they will leave no witnesses behind. There'll be hair on the walls, Dick promises Perry.

The mastermind of the crime, Dick, is also a competent auto mechanic. He provides the car as well as the gun. Together, the two men purchase the remainder of the necessary items.

In order to spend a night away from his family, with whom he lived as a condition of his parole, Dick establishes an alibi. He lies to them, saying he is going to Fort Scott with Perry, who is to get some money from his sister. At a later time, when the evidence mounts against the two, it is revealed that Perry does not even know where his sister lives.

Certain other clues to the identity of the murderers are missed at first. When Dick and Perry stop at a Garden City gas station, something about the two men disturbs the attendant. Yet, after the tragedy he does not connect the "tough customers" with the event; further, Dick's parents not only fail to catch Dick's lies, but are unobservant of numerous stealthy acts. All these points come together later when the police begin to track Perry and Dick.

Following the suspenseful technique he has used throughout the first part of the narrative, Capote leaves Perry and Dick in "the moon-illuminated night" as the car moves toward the Clutter house. At this point no description of the actual crime follows. We learn nothing about the way it happened until much later when the men are caught and confess.

The remainder of the night is passed over, and then it is a beautiful Sunday morning. Nancy Ewalt, a friend of Nancy Clutter, is driven to River Valley Farm because it is customary for her to go to church with the Clutter family. When nobody answers the door, the Ewalts leave and go to Susan Kidwell's apartment, for Susan, Nancy's closest friend, also goes to church every Sunday with the Clutters. Mr. Ewalt drives the girls back to River Valley Farm and they go inside the house. There is a strange stillness. When they see Nancy's purse lying open on the floor, they know something is wrong. The door to Nancy's room stands open and sunlight floods the room. Inside they find their friend dead.

When the sheriff arrives at the scene, he discovers all the family has been killed. Nancy is lying in her bed, her hands and ankles tied; a shotgun held next to her head had killed her. Next, the body of Mrs. Clutter is found in her room; she, too, had been bound and shot. In the basement are two more bodies; like the others Kenyon had been tied with rope, but also his mouth was covered with adhesive tape, and "he'd

been shot in the face, directly head-on." The last body
found is Mr. Clutter's, his the bloodiest, for not only
had he been shot but also his throat had been cut.
Tape was wound around his mouth and head. Some
cord dangles from a pipe overhead, where at some
point Mr. Clutter had been strung up. We learn much
later that Mr. Clutter was the first to be killed, and
his wife the last.

The bodies are taken away in ambulances, the
relatives are notified, and the family that had been
expected to be together for Thanksgiving begins to
gather instead for "a mass burial."

The criminals are seen only once again in this
section; the concluding segment gives one paragraph
to each. Perry is asleep at midday in a hotel room,
his boots in a basin of water that has a pinkish color.
This detail represents another clue that will eventually be used in evidence, the boots having left a
bloody footprint on a box next to Mr. Clutter's body.
While Perry sleeps, Dick returns to his parents' farmhouse, where he eats Sunday dinner with the family.
Afterwards, to the amazement of his father, Dick falls
asleep while watching a football game, something
the father has never seen happen before. Capote adds
a grim reminder to the final sentence in Part I as he
explains that Mr. Hickock "did not understand how
very tired Dick was, did not know that his dozing son
had, among other things, driven eight hundred miles
in the past twenty-four hours." In the ironic statement,
the normally innocuous phrase "among other things"
becomes a note of horror.

Part II, "Persons Unknown," opens with a brief
description of the cleaning up of the house at River
Valley Farm by four of Herb Clutter's closest friends.
After working late into the afternoon, they gather together the visible reminders of the bloody event—pillow, bedclothes, mattresses, a couch—and burn them

in the north field of the farm, "a flat place full of color . . . the shimmery tawny yellow of November wheat stubble." The quiet beauty of the landscape on this lovely November day intensifies the horror of all that has happened. As one of the men watches the bonfire he thinks of the goodness and virtue of Herb Clutter, a man who had built a worthwhile life; and he cannot understand how all of that "could overnight be reduced to this—smoke, thinning as it rose and was received by the big, annihilating sky."

The same mournful tonal quality employed by Capote is to appear again in conjunction with land-scape when the criminals are caught and also at the conclusion of the book, when all the events set in mo-tion by Dick Hickock's scheme are over and the prin-cipal actors are dead.

Three different kinds of events seem to take place almost simultaneously as this segment of the story un-folds. The investigative procedures begin immediately with the appointment of Alvin Dewey of the Kansas Bureau of Investigation and his three special agents. The Clutters are buried after memorial services at-tended by a thousand people. Meanwhile, the mur-derers buy a large number of "salable pawnable" items—jackets, slacks, shirts, diamond rings, a gold wristwatch, cufflinks, cameras, television sets. Every-thing is purchased by checks written by Dick, checks that will begin to "bounce" not long after the two men leave the state. Dick, the con artist, has no trouble persuading salespeople to accept his checks. The only thing that concerns him is the knowledge that his parents will suffer when the checks are stopped for nonpayment.

Nevertheless, the two men leave Kansas City for Mexico, their pockets filled with cash and the car crammed with possessions. It is exactly a week since the murders took place. In the car is a small Zenith radio, one of the few things they had gained from the crime. Although the Clutters' housekeeper discovers the loss immediately and points it out to the chief investigator, Dewey cannot believe "the family had been slaughtered for paltry profit." The terrible irony is that they were. Dick's information and calculations were completely wrong, but once he and Perry discovered that, there was no turning back for them.

In Mexico, Dick and Perry sell the grey portable radio as well as a pair of binoculars that belonged to Herb Clutter. Further irony is that the purchaser is a Mexico City policeman.

The day the two men begin their trip to Mexico, another event involving the remaining members of the Clutter family takes place. It is reported "on the social page" of the local newspaper: the marriage of Beverly Clutter and Vere Edward English. Capote notes that the wedding was a "full-scale social affair" in which the bride wore white, and music was provided by a soloist and organist. Carefully choosing his words to underscore the callousness of the action by one of the two heirs of the double-indemnity insurance policy in addition to the remainder of the estate, Capote writes that the ceremony took place in "the church in which, three days earlier, the bride had formally mourned her parents, her brother, and her younger sister." By next quoting certain details from the newspaper, he underscores a story of frugality and practicality. "Vere and Beverly had planned to be married at Christmastime. The invitations were printed and her father had reserved the church for that date. Due to the unexpected tragedy and because of the many relatives being here from distant places, the young couple decided to have their wedding Saturday." The reader recalls Hamlet's line about the swift marriage of his mother following upon the death of his father; Hamlet's friend, Horatio, tells him he came to Elsinore "to see your father's funeral." Hamlet responds, requesting Horatio not to mock him, for surely "it was to see my mother's wedding." When Horatio notes that one quickly followed the other, Hamlet speaks the famous words: "Thrift, thrift, Horatio. The funeral-baked meats / Did coldly furnish forth the marriage tables."

In Mexico, it is not long before Perry and Dick are down to their last few dollars, even the money Dick got from the sale of the car. Dick refuses to take a job as an auto mechanic in Mexico because of the low wages, and he buys two bus tickets to return to the United States. As the second part of the story ends, the two men have gone from Mexico to California, where they are attempting to hitch a ride in the Mojave Desert. Although they are planning to rob and kill the driver who picks them up, the right set of circumstances does not present itself, and they commit no further murders.

In the opening pages of Part III, "Answer," Floyd Wells, Dick's former cellmate in Kansas State Penitentiary, is introduced. It was through Wells that Dick had learned about the Clutters and River Valley Farm. During the time they spent together discussing jobs they'd had, Wells had talked about working for Herb Clutter some years before and about the large, expensive operation Clutter ran. Dick, fascinated by everything involving the Clutters, constantly asked questions about them; he wanted to know each detail of their lives. Soon Dick reached the point where he said that when he and Perry got out of prison they were going to rob the Clutters and kill anybody who was there. At the time, Wells thought it was "just talk," and he did not believe Dick.

However, one night in his cell (he was not released as early as the other two), Wells hears a radio broadcast about the Clutter murders and knows im-

mediately that Dick had been involved. Although it
takes Wells some days to gather the courage to tell his
story to the warden, he finally does it.

Wells's action provides the lead Dewey has been
seeking. The very night he obtains information and
photographs of Smith and Hickock, he sends one of his
investigators, Harold Nye, to the Hickock farmhouse
to learn what he can about Dick's activities. The Hick-
ocks, unsuspecting of their son's role in the murders,
talk freely about Dick's life, their dislike of Perry
Smith, the trip that Dick took one weekend with
Perry to Fort Scott to see Perry's sister, and his unusual fatigue on his return. In the corner of the room
is a shotgun, Dick's. It is the gun which killed the Clutters, as is eventually shown in the trial. Nye elicits all
the information he can from the family, but never
tells them that Dick is a suspect in a murder case.

As the two criminals make their way back to
Kansas—against Perry's wishes—the investigation goes
on in different places. In Las Vegas, Nye finds the
rooming house Dick and Perry had stayed in before
going to Mexico; later, in San Francisco, he interviews
Perry's sister, who has not seen her brother for four
years. The most important information Nye gains is
that the sister never lived in Fort Scott; in fact, she
had never been to Kansas.

Driving a car they steal in Iowa, Perry and Dick
return briefly to Kansas, where Dick once again raises
money by passing bad checks. Although Dewey learns
very quickly about the checks and the stolen car, he
cannot catch up with Perry and Dick, who, with the
money Dick has accumulated, drive south to Florida
shortly before Christmas. But within a week of their
arrival in Miami they run out of money, and soon they
are on the road again. In the port of Galveston the two
men try to get work on freighters leaving the country,
but they fail because they have neither papers nor

passports. They return to Las Vegas in their stolen car, stopping briefly at the post office there for Perry to pick up the package of clothing—including boots— that he had shipped back from Mexico. As they drive off towards their old rooming house, two policemen recognize the license plates and description of the car. "The long ride" of Smith and Hickock, ten thousand miles in six weeks, is over.

At the Las Vegas city jail, the men are kept in different cells and are interrogated separately. When the detectives reveal to Hickock that they have a footprint and the boots that made them, he finally breaks, telling them that Perry was the murderer who "killed them all." Smith is less pliable. The detectives can get no confession from him while he is in the Las Vegas jail. But on the way back to Kansas, when Dewey repeats something confidential that Perry had told Dick, Perry yields at last, telling the entire story of the night at the Clutter home. However, Perry's version of the events differs significantly from Dick's. Where Dick blamed Perry for all the murders, Perry claims that Dick killed the mother and daughter. Later, before the first trial, Perry takes the blame for all the slaughter, telling Dewey he is doing it because he feels sorry for Dick's mother. Dewey, who is never certain about this point, does not allow Perry to alter the original confession.

Perry shows himself to be a strange, psychopathic mixture of vicious killer and compassionate protector. He had given Mrs. Clutter a chair to sit on, put a pillow under Kenyon's head, kept Dick from raping Nancy. It all seemed like a dream, he tells the investigators, unreal, with himself watching to see how it ended. He thought Mr. Clutter "a very nice gentleman. Soft-spoken. I thought so right up to the moment I cut his throat."

As the two men are being brought to the Garden

City jail, a crowd that "might have been expecting a parade" waits: newsmen, photographers, television cameramen, mothers with babies, students calling out cheerleader lines, Boy Scouts, members of a bridge club, people eating hot dogs and drinking pop. Among the crowd is Capote; like the other people in Garden City, he is getting his first look at Hickock and Smith, with whom he is to become well acquainted over the next few years.

Darkness falls before the criminals arrive, and soon the crowd shrinks in number to a few hundred people, witnesses who see the men taken inside. The square soon empties. In a scene that might have come from an earlier Capote novel, only two stray tomcats are left in the dark chill night. The "miraculous autumn weather" that had lasted up to that moment, was over: "the year's first snow began to fall."

Part IV, "The Corner," the final section of the work, is the least absorbing. Unavoidably, it lacks the suspense of the preceding chapters. For five years Smith and Hickock are kept in jail until their death by hanging, and Capote reports on the period in much detail, too much, about witnesses, testimony, legal skirmishes, psychiatric testing which should have been given but wasn't, and crimes of other prisoners who were on Death Row at the same time as Dick and Perry.

A series of events before the trial makes the outcome inevitable. Although the court-appointed attorneys for the defense ask for psychological testing of their clients, the judge denies it, permitting only examination by physicians in general practice; they find the defendants sane, as understood by most laymen. Further, one day before the trial begins, the Clutter estate is auctioned off, an inflamatory reminder of the crime; finally, at least one juror clearly in favor of capital punishment is selected for the jury. The jury takes forty minutes to reach the verdict, which carries with it the death penalty.

The two men are transferred to the Kansas State Penitentiary in Lansing, where they are put on Death Row. They have been sentenced to die in May, 1960, but an appeal for a new trial stays the execution. During the years that follow, Dick's father dies of cancer, and his mother loses the farm, so that she is forced to live with relatives. Time passes slowly for the men as they wait alone in their tiny, empty cells through the long, cold winters and hundred-degree summers. There is no work, nor exercise. All they can do is read.

Dick spends much of this time writing letters. One result of this activity is to bring about a hearing to determine whether he and Perry had been given a fair trial. When the decision goes against them, a new date is set for their execution. This time a federal judge grants a reprieve. More appeals are followed by more stays of execution. Three times the case is taken to the Supreme Court of the United States, but in each instance the Court refuses to hear it. At last, time runs out for Smith and Hickock; they die on the gallows April 14, 1965: Hickock brave and cool, and Smith apologetic for what he has done.

The concluding chapter of the story reveals most fully Capote's sympathy for Perry Smith, something apparent throughout the entire work. However, the author's feelings for Hickock are very different, and Capote makes no attempt to balance the amount of information he provides about Dick. We learn a great deal about Perry and little about Dick. The worst elements of Dick's nature are described, so that he becomes an unattractive character whom the reader cannot like. From first to last, Capote shows Dick as a fast-talking, self-centered, shallow, small-time crook. Almost the only part of Dick's life that becomes him is the leaving of it.

Although both Perry and Dick grew up in deprivation, that is, poverty, Dick had everything one associates with ordinary existence. He had a family that loved him, protected him, and defended him; there was a place to which he belonged, where he had lived all during his youth. He went to school in one area; he had the chance to make friends; he was married—twice—and had three sons. Yet none of this prevented him from becoming a criminal.

When Dick and Perry become allies they appear to be very much alike. Both are intelligent, close in age (Dick, twenty-eight; Perry, thirty), fastidious, tattooed, and maimed. Dick's face, as the result of an automobile collision, seems to have "mismatching parts." Perry's legs are mutilated from a motorcycle accident, so that he is misshapen and very small.

In actuality, the two are complete opposites. Dick never questions his own motivation, whereas Perry believes something is wrong with both of them, particularly himself. Thinking of all that happened to his family he cannot conceive he has escaped from the horror: a mother who strangled to death on her own vomit during an alcoholic binge; a sister who jumped from a hotel window; a brother who killed himself after driving his wife to suicide. Only one sister, whom he hates, and his father are left. Except for a postcard from his father to the warden when he is on Death Row, in his last years there is no communication between Perry and his family; neither his father nor his sister makes any attempt to see him during the long period he is in prison.

Although Perry is shown to be the killer of at least two members of the Clutter family and probably all four, Dick enjoys killing, as evidenced in an episode in which he is shown deliberately swerving his car to the side of the road to run down an old dog. On the other hand, Perry's violent acts are much more complex. He has "unreasonable anger," reactions that are "out of proportion to the occasion," according to his friend Willie-Jay. And long before Perry murders the Clutters, his friend warns him of his "dangerous anti-social instincts."

Perry had been in trouble from the age of eight. Earlier, his life was one of suffering. Born to a Cherokee Indian mother, Flo Buckskin, and an Irish father, Tex John Smith, both riders in the rodeo, Perry, his brother, and his sisters became victims of the parents. Once the Smiths had to give up riding because of numerous injuries, their lives were disastrous. There were terrible fights and soon Flo began to drink. The two separated, with Flo taking the children.

For a couple of years, Perry lived with his mother, who had become not only a drunk but also a whore. When he was seven he was put into a Catholic orphanage, where he hated "the Black Widows" and was hated in return as "a half-breed child." Constantly beaten for wetting his bed (the result of a kidney problem he carried with him all his life), he never overcame his "aversion to nuns. And God. And religion." Worse treatment came to him in a shelter run by the Salvation Army. There a nurse, who always called him "nigger," would punish him by putting him into a tub of freezing water and holding him under "till I was blue." After he became seriously ill with pneumonia, he was taken away by his father, with whom he lived until he joined the Merchant Marine at sixteen.

The years with his father were hard, years of wandering around the country in a "house car," a makeshift combination of home and automobile. School came to an end for Perry in third grade. The

two struggled to make a living and when he became
a teenager, Perry tired of the marginal existence,
wanting something more for himself and feeling un-
appreciated by his father. "It would have been o.k.,"
Perry asserts, "if only I hadn't grown up." In a blaze of
anger the last time he saw his sister, years before the
Clutter murders, he blamed his lack of education on
his father, who prevented him from going to school
when he wanted to. Perry says of his father: "I was
his nigger. . . . Somebody he could work their guts
out and never have to pay them one hot dime." Yet
hatred and anger contend with the sense of childlike
loss Perry feels about his father. When Perry and Dick
first meet as cellmates at Kansas State Penitentiary,
Perry cries in his sleep about his father: "Dad, I been
looking everywhere, where you been, Dad?"

All his life Perry feels like a deserted child, even
though he was the only one to live with his father
after the breakup of the family. Because he couldn't
get along with his father, he joined the service. At
twenty-three, however, his career came to an end
with the motorcycle accident that crippled his legs.
After half a year in a hospital and another half spent
with an Indian friend and his family, Perry rejoined his
father in Alaska, where Tex Smith was building a
hunting lodge. Together they completed "quite an ex-
ceptional place," but few tourists came and the project
was a failure. The father gradually began to turn on
the son, taking out his disappointment on Perry, even
threatening him with a gun. One night when Perry
went for a walk, the father threw his possessions into
the snow and locked him out. Following that Perry
started "down the highway" with no money and no
plans. The highway led eventually to murder.

After working at odd jobs for a couple of years,
he committed a burglary in Kansas with a man he met
on his travels. Although they were arrested, they broke

out of jail, stole a car, and headed east. Within the year, however, the FBI caught up with Perry. Sentenced in 1956 to five to ten years in the penitentiary, Perry went to the prison where he encountered his nemesis, Dick.

Perry, who trusts almost nobody, begins to doubt Dick very quickly. Yet, he continues to admire some of his traits. To him, Dick is "totally masculine," a real man, something Dick himself strives to emphasize constantly. Always ready with a dirty joke or a boast about his prowess with women, Dick seems to have a need to prove his maleness to Perry. In Mexico, Dick has intercourse with a girl in a hotel room while Perry lies on the next bed.

But there is an element in Dick's carnality that disgusts Perry. To the psychologically oriented reader, that part of Dick confirms the idea of his sexual insecurity: Dick likes little girls. During the time the two men are out of prison, Perry acts as a watchdog over the young girls they meet. Dick masks his perversion by always stressing his normalcy, insistent that "most real men had the same desires he had." Thus he hides the sickness behind his seduction of "eight or nine" adolescents a few years before he was sent to the penitentiary.

Several reviewers have referred to the latent homosexuality in Perry and Dick's relationship and have faulted Capote's softening of that issue, seeing it as a clue to understanding the motivation of the criminals. Most critics agree that the men were death-obsessed, and one speaks of the interest we have in those who "murder as a substitute for sexual expression, as stemming from sexual and emotional deficiency." [4]

Reticent though Capote is on the matter, some of the homosexual episodes involving Perry are mentioned. Perry says: "But the queens on ship wouldn't leave me alone. A sixteen-year-old kid, and a small kid. . . . they get together and gang up on you. . . . It can make you practically want to kill yourself." Perry also blames his failure to be promoted in the Army on a homosexual sergeant.

For a brief time, in Mexico, Perry and Dick are supported by a German lawyer vacationing in Acapulco. Although the man already has a male companion, he pays the bills of the other two men as well. Intrigued by the men, he does numerous sketches of them, and when he leaves he gives Perry the sketchbook of drawings, which include "nude studies" of Dick.

Capote does not pursue this theme. He is more interested in Perry's family, his childhood, his suffering, his dreams.

When Perry was seven, an abused child in the orphanage, he had a dream that was to recur for the remainder of his life: a large, life-size, yellow parrot came as an avenger, and after blinding the nuns, eating their eyes, and killing them, "gently lifted him, enfolded him, winged him away to 'paradise.'" The bird stayed with him, as an avenger against all those Perry considered his tormentors, and after each incident there would be the ascent afterwards to paradise. When he is imprisoned after the murders, he dreams of committing suicide and of being carried away to freedom by the great yellow bird.

In many ways Perry is an attractive figure. He is talented musically and artistically; he sings, plays the guitar, and paints rather well. A dreamer, like a child who has not grown up, he collects maps, and fantasizes about pirate wrecks and buried treasure. Because he feels deprived of schooling, he attempts to educate himself; he reads, he studies, he makes long vocabulary lists to memorize. Lonely, he saves all the letters and cards he receives, carrying them with him from place to place.

Capote's strong sympathy for Perry comes in great measure from a certain identification with him; the child who dreamed of being famous, a great entertainer; the man who would always be the size of a twelve-year-old (Capote himself is very small); the deserted child; the lonely boy; the misfit in society. The rapport would explain the author's inclusion of large segments of psychiatric papers in the final portion of the novel. A physician describes Perry as a man who grew up "without direction, without love," someone who expects betrayal. His violence comes out of his past, his "now unconscious, traumatic experiences." Like other murderers, Perry suffered "severe emotional deprivation," an uncertain family life, cruelty from those around him.

In an article by three psychiatrists, there is reference to the activation of the murderous impulse when the criminal "unconsciously" sees an individual "as a key figure in some past traumatic configuration." The narrator asks who it is that Perry destroys psychologically in the first murder, that of Mr. Clutter. Is it "his father? the orphanage nuns. . . . the hated Army sergeant? the parole officer . . . ? One of them, or all of them."

If we are to take the psychological view, Perry has been doomed from birth. He, himself, provides part of the answer to the question society always raises about the murderer. Why did he do it? The Clutters did nothing to harm him. Perry states: "Like other people. Like people have all my life. Maybe it's just that the Clutters were the ones who had to pay for it."

Perry Smith and Richard Hickock pay on the gallows the toll imposed by society for their acts.

The story ends; in some ways the conclusion is like that of a Victorian novel, with all the characters accounted for, "deaths, births, marriages." More significantly, it is finished in quintessential Capote style, reminding the reader of *The Grass Harp, Breakfast at Tiffany's,* and "A Christmas Memory."

One May afternoon in Kansas "when the fields blaze with the green-gold fire of half-grown wheat," Dewey goes to the cemetery to visit his father's grave. Nearby are the graves of the Clutters, where he encounters Nancy Clutter's friend Susan Kidwell, now a young woman, a junior in college. They talk for a while, and as Susan leaves, Dewey envisions the way Nancy might have been, had she lived. The conclusion has Capote's memorable elegiac note. Dewey starts for home, going past the large trees, "leaving behind him the big sky, the whisper of wind voices in the wind-bent wheat."

Although some reviewers have criticized the ending as unfitting for a journalistic work, one must remember that this story is not purely documentary. Therefore, the ending seems completely appropriate to the artistic intent behind the novelistic element. Readers, left with a weight of sadness and loss, recognize that they have been confronted not only with an American tragedy but also the human tragedy, the wanton as well as the inexplicable nature of existence.

9

The Unforgivable Sin:
Answered Prayers

Capote's work, by his own description, is now in its
fourth cycle, one that began after the completion of
In Cold Blood. Thus far, it has been the least produc-
tive period of the writer's life. His only published book,
The Dogs Bark, is a selection from pieces written in
earlier times. An occasional travel essay appears, such
as the one about a visit to Martinique, "Music for
Chameleons," which was printed in *The New Yorker*,
September 17, 1979; the writing reminds one of *Local
Color*. There is even a line about California fruit
which might have been taken from the "Hollywood"
essay in *Local Color*. "Music for Chameleons" is ap-
pealing in the ways the earlier travel pieces are. There
is nothing in it, however, to suggest a new phase in
the writer's work. Nevertheless, it is the title of Capote's forthcoming book.

It is in the fiction of 1975–76 that changes are evident, a handful of short stories from the decade of the
seventies. Unfortunately, the stories not only have
failed to add to Capote's stature as creative writer, but
they have eroded some of the positive response to his
other work. The pattern is a familiar one in America,
and Capote's career is a reminder of others.

At the height of his success, Capote told people
he was working on a new novel, entitled *Answered
Prayers*. Although four of the stories have been

printed, the complete novel has not yet appeared. Because the subject matter of the stories brought on a great furor, Capote refrained from publishing any more of that novel. Readers of an earlier Capote story might have anticipated the direction he was to take in *Answered Prayers*.

The January, 1974, issue of the *Ladies Home Journal* contained the story called "Blind Items," which the editor introduced as follows: "A master writer turns gossip into an art form with wicked but—he claims—true stories about the very rich and famous. Their names and identifying details have been changed, but can you guess who's who?" [1]

Capote then gives his own introduction. Speaking of the pleasure he gets from reading gossip columnists and praising the "only four readable ones left," [2] he deplores the demise of an old form of newspaper gossip called the "blind item." Originating in nineteenth-century Paris, Capote says, the stories were used by columnists to blackmail people. In America, although the intention was to entertain rather than to extort money, gossip columnists wrote blind items during the thirties and forties. (Capote does not make it clear whether he is speaking of nineteenth- or twentieth-century America, but presumably it is the former.) Taken by a sense of nostalgia, he has decided to attempt to revive the form. What follows are five vignettes, four of them sexual, and the fifth, a dog story. Three of the four sexual stories have a homosexual theme.

A year and a half after the publication of "Blind Items" parts of *Answered Prayers* were brought out. All of the short stories were printed in *Esquire:* "Mojave" (June, 1975); "La Côte Basque" (November, 1975); "Unspoiled Monsters" (May, 1976); and "Kate McCloud" (December, 1976). The publication of the stories brought unexpected repercussions for Capote.

His social standing changed, and he also became involved in some legal actions. Now, however, Capote is in the process of revising *Answered Prayers,* and Christopher Cerf, of Random House, Capote's publisher, states: "I predict that . . . Capote's *Answered Prayers* will be published sometime in the next decade." [3]

Reputedly, people on the international scene have recognized a number of the figures in the stories. Nevertheless, Capote maintains that a writer cannot be denied the use of "material he has gathered as the result of his own endeavors and observations." Inasmuch as the author has portrayed a number of men and women who are self-indulgent and destructive to others, and whose sexual behavior might meet with disapproval from Capote's reader, it is obvious why those of Capote's acquaintances, who think he has modeled characters after them, believe they have been maligned.

Recently, an interviewer for *Vogue* asserted that readers "are still licking their chops with anticipation" as they await the publication of *Answered Prayers.*[4] Unquestionably there is an audience for it, even beyond those who are familiar with the circle about which Capote writes and who are able immediately to identify characters. Furthermore, in many instances it is unnecessary for people to play a literary guessing game, because the names of numerous celebrities are undisguised. Both the living and the dead are treated unceremoniously.

The predominant motif is sexual. Intercourse, the frequency of the act, desire for it, and variations of practice are spoken of in colloquial and suggestive terms. Tales are told about socialites, artists, writers, photographers, movie stars, real and fictional people, in addition to some who might as well have been named. Lewd jokes are made about them. For example, in one story a conversation about their genitalia is said to have taken place between a well-known photographer and a world-famous actress. In the same story, an outstanding American novelist is referred to as "Lolita-minded," a man "usually grave and courtly under the double weight of uncertain gentility and a Jack Daniels hangover." And an entire group of women writers, French and American, are labeled "intellectual lesbians."

The general theme, sexual predilection, is much the same from story to story. There is a great deal of rambling in the narration. Characters appear and disappear without any clear purpose. Plot lines are introduced and dropped. The reader struggles to find point or meaning to stories and reluctantly comes to the conclusion that in some instances there isn't any.

The title of the novel *Answered Prayers* has been taken from words spoken by St. Teresa of Avila. Capote paraphrases: "More tears are shed over answered prayers than unanswered ones." Implicitly, Capote intends the moral behind the saying to relate to the desires of his characters. Inasmuch as the stories focus exclusively on sexual experiences, the moral applies to them: the fulfillment of sexual prayers brings only sorrow or disappointment.

Using the device of the frame—numerous tales contained in an extended narrative—Capote follows the technique employed in *The Thousand and One Nights, The Decameron,* and *The Canterbury Tales.* But the stories have little to do with character, as in *The Canterbury Tales,* and much to do with passion, as in *The Decameron.*

The first piece from the collection, "Mojave," has one major tale within a tale, but the general framework encompasses several unrelated parts. In the three later stories, a man named P. B. Jones is the narrator. "Mojave" does not fit that part of the pattern.

The predominant plot concerns a woman, Sarah,

who has had sexual problems in her marriage for years. Because of her unhappiness, she has sought help from a psychoanalyst. Although the analyst is not very attractive, the woman has allowed him to become her lover. She doesn't love him—she doesn't even like him; she loves her husband. Eventually the analyst and Sarah part, and that little story ends.

Sarah at thirty-six looks like twenty. Nevertheless, the husband keeps mistresses, and the devoted wife helps him to find them. It is her way of holding her husband, because the couple have not shared a bed since the birth of their second child. "She wanted to, but she couldn't," and she avoids any sexual overtures the husband makes towards her. George Whitelaw, the husband, is an unhappy man, his wife the "principal cause" of his "secret fatigue."

We learn very little of the two of them, except for a detail here and there. Sarah married George because he looked like her father, a man who had shot himself. The two live in elegance, surrounded by original sculptures and paintings. A mocha velvet couch, a silver ice bucket, and a table lacquered yellow to match the yellow lacquered floor are described more carefully than the people.

One night the couple stays home and George reminisces about a summer he spent years before, just after leaving Yale. He went to the Mojave Desert and while hitching a ride he met an old man who was also hoping a car would pick him up. The man, George Schmidt, then told his story to the young George. Thus the major tale within the tale.

Schmidt told Whitelaw he had been deserted by his wife, a former stripper named Ivory Hunter. He had not been married very long, nor had he known Ivory well when he married her. A cousin of Ivory, Hulga, introduced them, and within a month they were married. Soon, however, Hulga warned Schmidt that Ivory was having an affair with a young Mexican. When Ivory persuaded Schmidt that it was not true, they drove away from the camp in which they had been living in their trailer. But Schmidt didn't know that his wife's lover was hiding in the back of the trailer. In the desert the lovers left the old man stranded when he got out of the vehicle.

As George finishes telling Schmidt's story, he seems to take great relish in repeating the sexual details about Ivory, so that for a moment Sarah speculates whether Ivory is the kind of woman who would appeal to George. Sarah does not really want to provoke her husband's interest, however, and she assures him that he is attractive to many women and she will help him find somebody to replace the recent mistress who has given him up.

Everyone in the story is unhappy in love, even Sarah's hairdresser friend, Jaime. Jaime lives with his lover, Carlos, to whom he has been very generous; but when Jaime's cousin Angelita comes to town, Carlos falls in love and wants to marry her.

The disparate pieces of the story are brought together by the underlying concept: the object of one's desire, the beloved, never returns love, and the lover is destined to suffer in the frustration and loneliness of love. It is a major theme in the work of Carson McCullers, a writer to whom Capote has often been compared.[5]

In the second story, "La Côte Basque," a narrator named Jonesy is introduced. (He becomes a character in his own right in the last two stories.) We are again reminded of the frame story, for Jones's role of keeping things going is similar to that of The Host, Harry Bailly, in *The Canterbury Tales*.

"La Côte Basque" begins with a coarse joke in a cowboy bar in New Mexico. Immediately the scene shifts to New York City, where the narrator, Jonesy, and a friend, Lady Coolbirth, encounter each other and decide to lunch together, because Lady Coolbirth has a table reserved at Côte Basque, an elegant French restaurant. There the two spend a long, gossipy afternoon over exquisite food and expensive champagne, Roederer's Cristal.

Why the introduction and then the instant contrast? Because the differences are more apparent than real: a bar, a restaurant; two men, a man and a woman; a crude joke, vulgar jokes and bawdy stories. From the ocean to the prairie, Capote suggests, all are alike.

As is required in frame stories, the setting is chosen for flexibility. Here the restaurant provides the opportunity to introduce a large number of figures. Although some of them are fictitious, the majority are not. Lady Coolbirth tells stories about them and about people who are not present. At nearby tables people also gossip.

Ina Coolbirth regales Jonesy with anecdotes about Cole Porter, Princess Margaret, Sammy Davis, Jr., Joseph Kennedy, and others less known to the public. Seated at a table next to Jonesy and Lady Coolbirth are Gloria Vanderbilt Cooper and Mrs. Walter Matthau, who exchange secrets and stories about Charlie and Oona Chaplin, stories that Jonesy overhears. Many famous names are dropped as people come and go: Lee Radziwell and Jackie Kennedy; "Mrs. William S. Paley lunching with her sister, Mrs. John Hay Whitney."

As Lady Coolbirth talks, Jones, the narrator of the larger story, notices clothes (Mainbocher, Balenciaga), jewels ("cinnamon colored diamonds"), and a compact of "white enamel sprinkled with diamond flakes."

The afternoon begins to wane. At the next table, Mrs. Matthau rubs her fingers over "a fallen yellow rose petal." Soon she and Mrs. Cooper leave. Everyone has gone except Jones, Lady Coolbirth, and two others. Tables are being reset for the evening. Capote picks up the note of the fallen rose petal, in one of the few artistic touches in the story, as he has the narrator describe the "atmosphere" as one "of luxurious exhaustion, like a ripened, shedding rose, while all that waited outside was the failing New York afternoon."

The third and fourth published segments of *Answered Prayers,* "Unspoiled Monsters" and "Kate Mc-Cloud," are the longest and most rambling stories in the group. In both, the author repeats a great deal of gossip about people on the international scene for the past fifty years.

Clearly, Capote wants to identify himself with P. B. Jones, author, and narrator of the story. Midway through "Unspoiled Monsters" Jones talks about his unfinished book, *Answered Prayers.* Moreover, at the end we are informed by Jones that he is beginning to write "Mojave." What is less clear is Capote's reason for the clue or for the biographical details laced into the story. Jones is monstrous, and, by his own admission, corrupt. He does anything; everything he has is for sale, and he makes his way by prostitution of one kind or another.

Born of unknown parents who abandoned him in a St. Louis vaudeville theater, P. B. Jones was raised by nuns in an orphanage. When he ran away at fifteen, he met a homosexual named Ned, who took him to Miami Beach and taught him the trade of masseur, something that was to be of great value many years later. Ned was not the first of Jones's male lovers. He informs us he was introduced to sex at the age of eight, a statement that fits in with Capote's actual experiences. Among P. B.'s early lovers were a priest and a Negro gardener. Jones makes it clear from the beginning that nobody and no calling are free from sexual corruption.

In picaresque fashion, Jones goes from one adventure to another. He meets a widow who gives him ten thousand dollars. Then he goes to New York. In the description of his arrival in the city there are brief touches of the old Capote style; again the passage contains autobiography, this time reminiscent of *Local Color.* It is October and as Jones watches from the bus window the city appears to glitter with promise, "cold and fiery in the rippling shine of a tumbling autumn sun."

Soon after Jones settles in New York he marries a girl he meets in Martha Foley's creative writing class, at Columbia University. She is "bloodless" looking, a "fishbelly-pale amazon with roped yellow hair and egglike eyes." Her name is Hulga. Is this the Hulga of "Mojave," the story which Capote had published the year before but which Jones is going to write soon? We seem destined not to know. Although the marriage fails and Hulga goes back to Minnesota with her parents, the two remain married. What Capote wants the reader to know is that Hulga is not Flannery O'Connor's heroine ("Good Country People"), just another Hulga. Nevertheless, the allusion evokes the same clumsy, graceless woman of the earlier story.

Jones, who is trying hard to get his fiction published, at the age of twenty becomes friendly with Turner Boatwright, "Boaty," a man described as the possessor of "crotch-watching eyes." Boaty is fiction editor of a woman's magazine, but is reluctant to publish anything of Jones's, even though they become lovers. Jones describes the brief seduction scene in a way that makes it sound like an off-color joke. Eventually, Boaty helps Jones rewrite a story and then publishes it.

Through his lover, Jones enters a different kind of world. In Boaty's home he meets world-renowned photographers, composers, movie stars, artists, dancers, the social elite, whose faces and activities keep numerous papers and magazines solvent. And there he meets the woman Kate McCloud, whose name is mentioned at intervals throughout this story and who will be—in a limited sense—the subject of the next one.

Kate wears a wristwatch given to her by John Kennedy. Although readers are titillated by the mention of Kennedy and are led to speculate about the "real" Kate, they never learn about Kate's relationship to Kennedy; but some of the biographical details of her life are an intriguing mixture of facts from the lives of the Kennedys, the Bouviers, and the Onassises. Jones refers to the intense love he has for Kate, yet has no hesitation in describing her promiscuity in a lewd joke. Many years later, he tells a friend that *Answered Prayers* is not about Kate McCloud and her "gang" but they are in it.

In his odyssey, Jones leaves Boaty to live with Alice Lee Langman, "the first lady of letters in America." Jones's interest is really in Miss Langman's agent, her publisher, and her connections. He despises her and makes it apparent in his discussions of her sexual habits. However, through Miss Langman's help he gets a Guggenheim, a grant from the National Institute of Arts and Letters, and a publisher's advance for stories. When the stories are published, they are ignored, in spite of the fact that Miss Langman reviews them. Jones, bitterly disappointed, leaves her.

Jones's next lover, Denny Fouts, has been kept by some of the wealthiest men in the world. Also, Jones states, Fouts was "impaled" in the work of two writer friends, Gore Vidal (with whom Capote has been feuding for a long time) and Christopher Isherwood. When Denny invites P. B. to Paris at his expense, he sails there on the Queen Elizabeth. Denny becomes ill and goes to a famous clinic, and a short time after leaving there he dies.

Denny provides the narrator of "Unspoiled Monsters" another opportunity to gossip about famous men and their sexual habits: a cosmetics tycoon, unnamed, but identifiable through certain clues; an elderly director of Dutch Petroleum; and King Paul of Greece. Naughty stories about Denny lead to similar spin-offs about other notables; Jones speaks of heiresses who bought the same husband (at different times) because of his reputed prowess in bed. And he also gives advice for those who want help sexually, going into some detail about "an Oriental trick" he calls "karezza."

Although Jones does not like Paris, he enjoys meeting the people who reside there, some of them very well known American expatriates. At a favorite bar he becomes friendly with Camus, Natalie Barney,[6] and Alice B. Toklas, whom he calls Gertrude Stein's "widow." Through Miss Barney, Jones is invited to tea at Colette's home. Suddenly we are back in Capote's essay, "The White Rose." Many of the details are the same—the description of Colette, with her darkly outlined eyes, lipsticked mouth, and whitely powdered face. In both, Colette meets the twenty-four-year-old writer in her bedroom, a room filled with a marvelous collection of paperweights. In both, Colette describes one for him, the White Rose, an antique. The date of the weight varies; in "The White Rose" it is 1842, in "Unspoiled Monsters," 1850. In the later story, the paperweight is specifically said to have been made by the Clichy factory, whereas in the earlier anecdote, Colette calls it a Baccarat piece.

There is, however, one very significant difference between the two stories. In the earlier one, Colette comments about Cocteau's remark about Capote,

whom he had described as looking like a ten-year-old
angel but possessing a very wicked mind. In "Unspoiled Monsters" Colette asks Jones what he wants
from life, besides being rich and famous. He answers
that he wants "to be a grown-up person." But Colette
tells Jones that can never be for anyone; people have
only moments when they are grown-up. We all carry
a child inside of us, no matter who we are. "Death,"
she says, sends the child "scuttling and leaves what's
left of us simply an object, lifeless but pure, like The
White Rose." She gives Jones the paperweight as a reminder of the difference between life and art. No such
importance is attached to the weight Colette gives
Capote in "The White Rose," for Colette calls it
merely a souvenir of the visit, in spite of its monetary
value.

The reader feels compelled to pursue the matter of Capote's intent in repeating and significantly
altering the Colette story in "Unspoiled Monsters."
The lovely vignette is jarringly out of place, not because it has nothing to do with the main thread of
the narrative—there is none—but because this is a different kind of anecdote, with no gossip, no humor, no
sex. Has Capote forgotten he told it before? Surely
not. Here, he places it about midway in the story.
Throughout, he has been using two time periods,
Jones as a young man and Jones at thirty-six. The
Colette episode occurred when Jones was twenty-four.
Jones in time present, at thirty-six, is at the low point
of his life. He has been involved in something disastrous, important enough to get into the newspapers.
What it is we never learn. Jones, now back in New
York and down on his luck, meets a friend with whom
he gets drunk; they begin to discuss Jones's unfinished
work. The friend says, "So you're writing again.
Novel?" Jones tells his friend, who is "there with all
the garden-party queries," that the unfinished book is

really more "a report" or "an account" than a novel, and it is entitled *Answered Prayers*. The subject matter of it is "Truth as illusion." Some philosophical introspection then takes place on the nature of truth and illusion, and the segment ends.

The juxtaposition of the Colette story and of the discussion about *Answered Prayers* provides the key to Capote's repetition of details from "The White Rose." In the last decade, Capote has stressed one point on numerous occasions in interviews. That is, the artist uses what he has, what is available to him. In a sense he is only a vehicle. The Colette episode makes a clear distinction between art and artist. The artist is merely human, nothing more than a "smutty little boy," but art is everlasting, "durable and perfect." Thus the story may be seen as Capote's defense of fiction.

In "Unspoiled Monsters" the Colette story takes place when the fictional character Jones first goes to Paris. He remains in Europe twelve years, traveling, writing, meeting many people. His writing doesn't go well, and he has problems getting published.

For a time Jones winters in Tangier, where he meets the novelist Jane Bowles. Jones thinks Mrs. Bowles a genius, as does Capote, who once wrote an introduction for her short stories.

Tangier was also one of the homes of Woolworth heiress Barbara Hutton in those days. In an exotic segment of the story, Jones describes the frail, sickly, much-married Miss Hutton and the setting in which she lived. It resembles something out of *The Arabian Nights,* from the enormous, crimson-turbaned, white-clothed servant at the gate, to the lantern-lighted trees, to the rooms filled with delicate ivory screens, silk and satin brocaded pillows, brass tables, and magnificent oriental rugs.

Upon meeting Jones, Miss Hutton tells a friend,

Aces Nelson, that Jones can be of help to Kate Mc-
Cloud. Jones returns to Paris to be introduced to Kate
by Aces. But first he must listen to the story Aces has
to tell about her.

Kate Mooney was the beautiful young daughter
of an Irish immigrant when she married Harry Mc-
Cloud, scion of a rich, well-educated, sophisticated
family. Through the McCloud family's efforts, Kate
became a sophisticated, knowledgeable woman of the
world. However, the marriage was a failure because
Harry was a disturbed man, paranoid in his feelings
about Kate. Because her husband was dangerously
violent, Kate said, she divorced him. Some time later,
she married the richest man in Germany. There is
more to come about Kate in the next story.

As "Unspoiled Monsters" ends we are back in
time present. Jones has become a male prostitute—
that detail is woven in at several points as the narrative moves from one time period to another. Whatever
happened between Jones and Kate McCloud is over,
but it is of recent vintage. He is writing again, as he
announced to the friend with whom he had the discussion about *Answered Prayers*. It is that friend,
somewhat surprisingly, who helped him obtain a job
as a prostitute for the sex agency, Self Service, when
he was in desperate financial straits. While living in
New York, at the Y.M.C.A., Jones is determined to
write the things he knows and remembers. He begins
"Mojave."

The last published story of *Answered Prayers*,
"Kate McCloud," is the least interesting and most tedi-
ous of the group. In style and pattern it resembles
the earlier pieces; once more P. B. Jones is the narrator who tells anecdotes about well-known people.

As the story opens in time present, Jones has
finished writing "Mojave." Restless and unhappy, he
goes to see an old movie, starring Montgomery Clift.

The movie takes him back in memory to the time he met Clift through Turner Boatwright, his "old mentor (and nemesis)." Jones tells several stories at that point about Dorothy Parker, Estelle Winwood, Tallulah Bankhead, and Montgomery Clift, stories which can only be categorized as vulgar.

Eventually Jones gets to the story of his meeting with Kate McCloud. It is a winter in Paris (the time is not given). Aces Nelson tells Jones that Kate has a psychosomatic spinal problem, an imaginary ailment brought on by her problems with her estranged second husband, the German industrialist. Because Jones is a masseur, he can help Kate. Further, says Aces, she needs a bodyguard and Jones can serve that role also.

The two men go to Kate's apartment, where she is serving tea to a friend in her bedroom. Once more, there is a considerable amount of gossip and chit-chat and some suggestive stories. It is amusing that Kate, in talking about a dinner party she went to, describes the Shah of Iran as telling "tasteless jokes," for that term, unfortunately, fits the greater part of the substance of *Answered Prayers*.

In the course of the afternoon Jones learns that Kate's husband has their five-year-old son and will not allow her to see him. There is talk of kidnapping. Soon everyone leaves except Kate and Jones. Jones gives Kate a massage, which provides the occasion for a description of the nude Kate and an unattractive story of Jones's arousal as he massages her. When Kate falls asleep, Jones kisses her ankle and leaves.

For no apparent reason, the time moves again briefly into the present, and Jones tells about his activities in the Self Service. The stories are sexually explicit and have no relationship at all to whatever there is to be said about Kate McCloud. Having worked in the New York episodes, the narrator again

shifts back to Paris, where Aces tells Jones that Kate
wants to hire him. A long and rambling story about
Kate's German husband and their marriage follows,
and Aces concludes by voicing concern for Kate's
safety.

Jones is pleased that Kate has selected him to
help her. He feels useful and happy. As he goes to
sleep he makes plans to buy a gun. But he has a
strange dream that night about himself, Kate, and her
son. They are at the beach, dressed in elegant clothing
out of an earlier period. The seascape, the people,
and the colors remind him of a beautiful painting.
Everything seems quiet and harmonious as the story
comes to an end with Jones's dream.

Perhaps because the story is so disjointed, the
characters so unbelievable, and the plot so foolish, the
reader finds "Kate McCloud" excessively long. Unlike
"Unspoiled Monsters," there is nothing to redeem this
last story. But one returns to "Unspoiled Monsters" to
try to fit puzzle pieces together.

For the critic, the most interesting aspects of "Unspoiled Monsters" are those in which Capote uses autobiographical information in describing the character
Jones. Because Capote wants to be identified with his
fictional creation, he gives to Jones part of his own history. There are the homosexual experiences as a child;
a trip to New York which produces the same effect on
both; educated male lovers who introduce them to
famous people. Both men are writers, even of the
same material, and they follow the same procedures,
writing in pencil in copybooks. Capote's story "Miriam" was published in the O. Henry Memorial Award
volume (1946), after appearing in *Mademoiselle*.
Jones's first story was reprinted in *Best American
Short Stories*. Later, disappointment and bitterness
result from the critical reception of both writers' work.

They are unable to finish their novel, *Answered Prayers*.

And there is more doubling. Capote lived in Europe for a number of years. So did Jones. Jones is praised by a friend for his portrait of Cecil Beaton, a popular Capote piece. When Jones speaks of himself "intellectually" as "a hitchhiker," one who picks up his education as he finds it, he might well be describing Capote. Then, there is the picture on the book jacket, the one, Jones tells us, is "the photograph of me Beaton had taken for Boaty's magazine and which I had used on the jacket of my book." What else could Capote be speaking of than his famous picture on the cover of *Other Voices, Other Rooms?* Jones says the photograph suggests an incorrect view of him, that of "a crystal lad, guileless, unsoiled, dewey, and sparkling as an April raindrop." Capote wants to disabuse anyone of the notion that he was an innocent at twenty-four. Finally, Capote is surely characterizing himself through Jones when the latter says: "I was a *born* bastard—a talented one whose sole obligation was to his talent." That is what Capote has been telling us directly and indirectly in the past decade.

"Unspoiled Monsters" has yet another tantalizing quality. It takes us back to a work Capote wrote almost thirty years earlier, "Shut a Final Door," one of Capote's best stories and far superior to those of recent vintage.

Walter Ranney, of "Shut a Final Door," and P B. Jones, of "Unspoiled Monsters" (as well as other stories in which Jones appears), have much in common in history and personality. Each one goes to New York and soon ingratiates his way into a wealthy social set and interesting work. Both Walter and P. B. use other people to get ahead, and later turn on them. Beneath all relationships lies a pattern of insincerity.

Neither man likes people. Walter knows he is incapable of loving, and the reader knows that to be the
case with P. B. Sexual affairs provoke hostile reactions in both men; hatred is the end result of each
encounter.

Significantly, certain characters in the two stories
also resemble each other. In the early story, Anna
Stimson, an editor with whom Walter is very close, is,
in all probability, Alice Lee Langman, lady of letters,
in "Unspoiled Monsters." The likenesses between Kurt
Kuhnhardt, in the first story, and Turner Boatwright,
in the second, is even more striking. Kuhnhardt, the
head of an advertising agency, is a man with a particular kind of reputation, an innuendo that suggests
he is homosexual; suggestion is completely abandoned in *Answered Prayers,* and the reader is told of
Boaty's homosexuality through episode and description. In both stories the young protagonist becomes
the "protégé" of the older man, and in both instances the parting is unfriendly. Each man takes new
lovers: Walter dreams of Kuhnhardt and his new
protégé laughing at him and closing him out; P. B.
has the satisfaction of remembering that Boaty was
viciously murdered in his townhouse by a "Puerto
Rican hustler."

Walter and P. B. are further linked by an interest in malicious and destructive gossip. Although
there are few examples of Walter's gossip, we are
aware that it leads to his loss of job, friends, and
"patron." P. B. gossips interminably and cruelly, but
he does not tell us what effect this has on his fate,
which is finally much like Walter's.

At the end, Walter is completely alone, without
work, and without money. He is in a hotel room that
has a window he cannot open, as if he were imprisoned. As he lies on the bed watching the turning

blades of the ceiling fan, he is filled with fear of discovery, discovery of the meaning of the voice on the telephone.

P. B. Jones, at the nadir of his existence, lives at the Y.M.C.A. "in a viewless second-floor cell." He thinks briefly of suicide. Instead, he tells his own story and also begins to write one. Jones has no need to hear the voice on the telephone, for in some of his more honest moments he recognizes he has met the enemy and he is himself. Like Walter he is caught in his own never-ending circle of destruction.

Resemblance creates another kind of circle. Jones is like Ranney, and Jones is pointedly Capote's stand-in. When we look at reality, that is, the writer's life, and compare it to his fiction, we find an ironic twist. It is life imitating art. Capote's world, at this juncture, seems to mirror Walter's. The doors have been shut; Capote has met Capote, someone he has known for a very long time.

To date there is only one other published Capote short story that has had wide circulation, the piece "Dazzle," which he has said will be part of a larger work. Even if the writer had not pronounced it autobiographical, many of the details would inform the reader of that. By now Capote's audience knows much about his early years, and "Dazzle" adds more information.

The middle-aged narrator—unquestionably Capote, with no persona this time—tells of a childhood episode involving his paternal grandmother. His parents were divorced at the time his grandmother made one of her infrequent visits to see him in New Orleans, where he was living with relatives. Although his grandmother was a poor schoolteacher in Florida and had little money, she sometimes wore a dazzling pendant which looked like a gem stone. It was actually a faceted rock crystal dyed yellow, but the necklace caused trouble.

A laundress, Mrs. Ferguson, known for her magical powers, covets the necklace. The little boy has a secret wish. Inasmuch as Mrs. Ferguson is famous for her ability to help people obtain their desires, he agrees to steal the necklace in exchange for the granting of his wish.

When he gives the necklace to Mrs. Ferguson and she asks him what he wants, he is reluctant to tell. He pretends that he longs to be a tap dancer. Mrs. Ferguson tells him that it is possible because he is so pretty. At that point he bursts out with the truth, telling her he wants to be changed into a girl. He is certain something is wrong with him.

Upset when she laughs at him, he tries to retrieve the necklace. Immediately, Mrs. Ferguson becomes furious. She begins to dangle the necklace in front of him so that it continually catches the light. He is put into a hypnotic state and appears to lose consciousness, for he has no awareness of the way he gets back home.

His grandmother and relatives are concerned about the loss of the necklace, but it is never recovered, nor does he ever tell anyone what happened. He is afraid, he asserts, if he mentioned Mrs. Ferguson she "might reveal what I'd told her, the thing I never told anyone again, not ever."

Many years pass. When the narrator is middle-aged, his grandmother dies. He didn't love her, yet he grieves. Instead of going to the funeral, however, or sending flowers, he gets drunk. He gets a call from his elderly father, who is furious at his behavior. The father curses him, saying his grandmother died "with your picture in her hand." After apologizing, the narrator hangs up, for he can never tell anybody of his guilt or of his inability to separate his grandmother from his memory of Mrs. Ferguson and what he wanted from her. He has never been able to come to terms with his secret feelings.

"Dazzle" differs not only from the recent fiction of Capote's but also from the earlier work. It is simply a little story, no more than that. A certain lifelessness permeates "Dazzle," and the story lacks the power of the confessional it intends to be. Nevertheless, "Dazzle" is only a very small segment of the promised book, which may reveal still another Capote.

The announcement by Random House of Capote's forthcoming book, *Music for Chameleons,* states that it is composed of fourteen pieces, including short stories, interviews, and conversations. Random House commends one particular selection as "the main offering," the story "Handcarved Coffins," subtitled "A Nonfiction Account of An American Crime."

During the year 1979, Andy Warhol's magazine *Interview* featured a series called "Conversations with Capote," a rather wide-ranging term to cover miscellaneous writings. "Handcarved Coffins" was the December, 1979 contribution to those "conversations." It is an account by Capote of an actual crime in a small western town.

Numerous murders are committed by a fanatical killer, who takes vengeance on townspeople for serving on a committee which voted to change certain river boundaries. In every case the slayer notifies his intended prey by sending each of them a miniature coffin which contains his or their photographs. Within a period of weeks or months after receipt of the grizzly warning, the victims are slain in some horrific way. Although the murderer is identified by an investigator, he is never brought to justice for lack of evidence.

Capote himself participates in this story, which contains a large amount of dialogue in a question and answer technique. Although "Handcarved Coffins" has been compared to *In Cold Blood,* there are only flashes here and there that remind the reader of the earlier work. "Handcarved Coffins" is suspenseful intermittently; few of the characters come to life. There is a strong flavor of sentimentality; and Capote's presence and musings add little to the work. It comes nowhere near the masterpieces of his earlier years.

Those who admire the short stories, the novels, the essays, the portraits, and the nonfiction novel of the first three cycles look forward to further Capote books. But whatever work is forthcoming, Capote's place in twentieth-century literature is secure. Capote, himself, has long since determined—as he must—that it is the work and not the opinions of a specific audience that matters. He made the point years ago when he quoted a favorite Arab saying of André Gide, one which served in part as the title of a book: "The dogs bark, but the caravan moves on."

Notes

1. THE MANY FACES OF TRUMAN CAPOTE: THE MAN AND THE WORK

1. David Halberstam's *The Powers That Be* (New York: Knopf, 1979).
2. Anne Taylor Fleming, "The Private World of Truman Capote," *New York Times Magazine*, 9 July 1978, p. 23.
3. There is some discrepancy in the date. The quotation is taken from Capote's essay, "Self-Portrait," which appears in *The Dogs Bark*, but he said in the Flem ing interview that he was nine when he left the South.
4. Capote dislikes having the critics refer to his stories as fantasy. He has stated he is concerned with psychological truths and apparently thinks a word such as fantasy lessens or changes the meaning. See Harvey Breit, *The Writer Observed* (Cleveland: World Publishing Company, 1956), p. 237.
5. Only the first job is mentioned by Capote over and over in interviews, probably because of its humor: he couldn't add.
6. The first explanation appears in Capote's "Self-Portrait," from *The Dogs Bark;* the second, in William Nance's, *The Worlds of Truman Capote* (New York: Stein and Day, 1970), p. 14; and the third, from the preface to the twentieth anniversary edition of *Other Voices, Other Rooms* (1967), reproduced as "A Voice from a Cloud" (1969), in *The Dogs Bark* (1973).

7.   Henry Rago, "The Discomforts of Storytelling," *The Sewanee Review* 56 (Summer 1948): 519.

8.   John Chamberlin, "Younger U.S. Writers," *Life*, 2 June 1948, p. 102.

9.   Truman Capote, "Truman Capote," *Vogue*, December 1979, p. 262.

10.   In *American Literary Scholarship*, 1971, James Justus, reviewing William Nance's *The Worlds of Truman Capote*, says that Capote's work won't "win any awards from the deep readers of the world," p. 268.

11.   (Garden City, New York: Doubleday & Co., 1957) pp. ix, x, 13.

12.   Capote, "Truman Capote," p. 311. The Mailer novels Capote speaks of are *The Armies of the Night, Of a Fire on the Moon,* and *The Executioner's Song.*

13.   Fleming, p. 25.

14.   *Esquire*, December 1979, pp. 30–34.

15.   Fleming, p. 23.

16.   Cathleen Medwick, "Interview," *Vogue*, December 1979, p. 311.

2.   THE LOST CHILD: *Other Voices, Other Rooms*

1.   Henry James's *The Turn of the Screw* is an instance of suggestion and possibility that becomes overt in *Other Voices, Other Rooms.*

2.   A reader is reminded of Tennyson's "Mariana," a poem filled with similar images of loneliness and death.

3.   There is an interesting similarity in the following passage from *Other Voices, Other Rooms* to the rape of Temple Drake in Faulkner's *Sanctuary*. "He did not move to touch her, but squatted, impotent at her side like a bereaved lover, like an idol . . . he bent close: 'He pushed that cigar in my belly-button, Lord in me was born fire like a child . . .' "

4.   John Aldridge calls it a metaphor for Skully's Landing. *After the Lost Generation: A Critical Study of*

the Writers of Two Wars (New York: Noonday Press, 1958), p. 214.

3. THE UNEXPLORED REALM: *A Tree of Night and Other Stories*

1. The reference is to "Children on Their Birthdays," which Ihab Hassan praises in *Radical Innocence: The Contemporary American Novel* (Princeton, N.J.: Princeton University Press, 1961), p. 239. Reviewer Milton Crane disliked it; see "Parade of Horribles," *Saturday Review of Literature,* 26 January 1949, p. 12.
2. *The Grass Harp* and *Breakfast at Tiffany's* fall under the first category.
3. Compare to Holly Golightly, in *Breakfast at Tiffany's*, who warns against loving those who travel in the sky.
4. Capote himself had such aspirations.
5. Jack Dunphy, Capote's closest friend, has spoken of his "beautiful articulate toes," in the interview with Anne Fleming, p. 25.
6. The color green is always important in Capote's stories. It is a major image in *Other Voices, Other Rooms*. Here it is used in connection with mirror-like toenails, a radio, and birds.
7. See the discussion of *Answered Prayers* in chapter 9.
8. "Capote and the Perrys," *Mademoiselle,* October 1967, p. 141. On other occasions Capote has said that "Miriam" is not one of his favorite stories, that it has too much of the "stunt" in it.
9. The image of the butterfly is important in the ending of "A Ride through Spain," in *Local Color*. After an upheaval created by passengers and soldiers on the train, calm is restored. As the train moves on again, butterflies blow in and out the windows, an emblem of the harmony and loveliness of nature.
10. Wind is used at the end of "Shut a Final Door" to indicate Walter's flight from reality. Wind is a

"nothing thing" which can remove him from the
horror of self-discovery.

11. Compare the images of the waves to those in the
conclusion of "Master Misery."

12. Note also the major image of "Shut a Final Door."

13. Capote uses this line from Job as part of his introduction to "The Headless Hawk," but it is appropriate for most of his "nocturnal stories."

14. In *Other Voices, Other Rooms* the eyes of Randolph,
Mr. Sansom, and the snake affect Joel at critical
moments.

15. Lilacs bleed "out the sockets of a skull."

4. PATHS OF MEMORY: *The Grass Harp*

1. There is a similarity in the description of the characters and the love relationship to those in *The Ballad
of the Sad Café* by Carson McCullers.

5. NEVER LOVE A WILD THING: *Breakfast at Tiffany's*

1. Alfred Kazin has the two different views, first in
The Open Form: Essays for Our Time (New York:
Harcourt, Brace, and World, 1961), p. 213; then
in *Bright Book of Life* (New York: Delta, 1974),
p. 209. Irving Malin prefers the earlier work; see
New American Gothic (Carbondale: Southern Illi-
nois University Press, 1962), p. 159. And Mark
Schorer praises the mood, in *The World We Imag-
ine: Selected Essays* (New York: Farrar, Straus,
1968), p. 294. For other comments on the novel, see
also: Walter Allen, *The Modern American Novel in
Britain and the United States* (New York: E. P.
Dutton, 1964); Alfred Kazin, *Contemporaries* (Boston: Little, Brown, 1962); and Ihab Hassan, *Radical
Innocence: The Contemporary American Novel*
(Princeton, N.J.: Princeton University Press, 1961).

2. *Playboy,* March 1968, p. 62.

3. Capote's love of paperweights dates back to a visit
    he paid Colette in Paris in 1947. She called them
    "snowflakes," which he interpreted to mean "dazzling
    patterns frozen forever." "The White Rose" appeared
    first in the *Ladies Home Journal,* July 1971, but is
    reprinted in the collection *The Dogs Bark* (New
    York: Random House, 1973).
4. Sadness and melancholy, as in Tennyson's "Tears,
    Idle Tears," when the poet is looking back "on the
    happy autumn fields / And thinking of the days
    that are no more."

6. SURPRISED BY JOY: STORIES OF THE FIFTIES AND SIXTIES

1. Capote seems to like three-year spans. When "A
    Diamond Guitar" opens, the story told has happened
    three years earlier.
2. Renaming a person one likes after someone she has
    cared for also occurs in *Breakfast at Tiffany's,* when
    Holly decides to call the narrator Fred because that
    is her brother's name.
3. The flaw, if one chooses to quarrel with "the given"
    of the story, is in Capote's seeming ignorance of
    Jewish customs. Belli, portrayed as an observant Jew,
    would never have had his wife buried in a non-
    sectarian cemetery.

7. PEOPLE, PLACES, AND THE CELEBRITY LIFE: THE NONFICTION PIECES

1. I use the term "Negro" rather than "black" because
    that is Capote's word.
2. Compare to Nathaniel West's *The Day of the Locust.*
3. In "A House of Flowers" Ottilie already has these.
4. It appeared earlier as "Truman Capote Introduces
    Jane Bowles," in *Mademoiselle,* December 1966,
    114–16.

5. Both "Maya Plisetskaya" and "A Gathering of Swans" (the commentary about Madame Agnelli and Mrs. Paley) appeared in *Harper's Bazaar;* the first sketch, September, 1959, pp. 182–83; the second, October, 1959, pp. 122–25.

6. Capote's travel piece "Fontana Vecchia" describes Gide in Taormina.

7. The arrangement is Capote's, following no chronology.

8. ACTS OF DARKNESS: *In Cold Blood*

1. "Bennett Cerf Remembers—I," *Publisher's Weekly,* 15 August 1977, p. 31.

2. A term used by Robert Langbaum in discussing Smith and Hickock, but one also used to describe the Satanic principle as it appears in such characters as Shakespeare's Iago. "Capote's Nonfiction Novel," from *Truman Capote's In Cold Blood: A Critical Handbook,* ed. I Malin (Belmont, Cal.: Wadsworth, 1968), pp. 117–18.

3. Melvin Friedman states that Capote admits to having invented the name Willie-Jay. "Towards an Aesthetic," from *Truman Capote's In Cold Blood: A Critical Handbook,* p. 167.

4. Langbaum, p. 117.

9. THE UNFORGIVABLE SIN: *Answered Prayers*

1. Page 81.

2. The four he names are Aileen Mehle (Suzy), Jack O'Brian, Joyce Haber, and Maxine Cheshire.

3. Leonore Fleisher, "Decade of the Big Deal: Publishing in the '70's," *Washington Post Book World,* 30 December 1979, p. 4.

4. Cathleen Medwick, *Vogue,* 1979, p. 263.

5. See especially Mark Schorer's "McCullers and Capote," in *The World We Imagine* (New York: Farrar, Straus and Giroux, 1968), pp. 274–96.

6. A biography of Miss Barney has recently been published. See Jean Chalon, *Portrait of a Seductress*, translated by Carol Barko (New York: Crown, 1979). Miss Barney was a lesbian and much of the book focuses on her sexual liaisons.

Bibliography

I. WORKS BY CAPOTE

A. *Books*

Other Voices, Other Rooms. New York: Random House, 1948.

A Tree of Night and Other Stories. New York: Random House, 1949. Contents: "Master Misery," "Children on Their Birthdays," "Shut a Final Door," "Jug of Silver," "Miriam," "The Headless Hawk," "My Side of the Matter," "A Tree of Night."

Local Color. New York: Random House, 1950. Contents: "New Orleans," "New York," "Brooklyn," "Hollywood," "Haiti," "To Europe," "Ischia," "Tangier," "A Ride through Spain."

The Grass Harp. New York: Random House, 1951.

The Grass Harp [A Play]. New York: Random House, 1952.

The Muses Are Heard. New York: Random House, 1956.

Breakfast at Tiffany's: A Short Novel and Three Stories. New York: Random House, 1958. Contents: "Breakfast at Tiffany's," "A Diamond Guitar," "The House of Flowers," "A Christmas Memory."

Observations. Photographs by Richard Avedon, commentary by Truman Capote. New York: Simon and Schuster, 1959.

The Selected Writings of Truman Capote. New York:

Random House, 1963. Contents: "A Tree of Night," "Miriam," "The Headless Hawk," "Shut a Final Door," "Children on Their Birthdays," "Master Misery," "A Diamond Guitar," "House of Flowers," "A Christmas Memory," *Breakfast at Tiffany's,* "Among the Paths to Eden," "New Orleans," "Ischia," "A Ride through Spain," *The Muses Are Heard,* "The Duke in His Domain," "A House on the Heights."

In Cold Blood. New York: Random House, 1966.

A Christmas Memory. New York: Random House, 1966.

The Thanksgiving Visitor. New York: Random House, 1967.

Trilogy, with Eleanor Perry and Frank Perry. New York: The Macmillan Company, 1969. Contents: Story, Script, and Notes of "Miriam," "Among the Paths to Eden," "A Christmas Memory."

The Dogs Bark. New York: Random House, 1973. Contents: "A Voice from a Cloud," "The White Rose," *Local Color,* "Fontana Vecchia," "Lola," "A House on the Heights," "Greek Paragraphs," *The Muses Are Heard,* "The Duke in His Domain," "Style: and the Japanese," *Observations* ("Isak Dinesen," "Mae West," "Louis Armstrong," "Jean Cocteau and André Gide," "Humphrey Bogart," "Ezra Pound," "Marilyn Monroe"), "Jane Bowles," "Cecil Beaton," "Ghosts in Sunlight: The Filming of *In Cold Blood,*" "Self-Portrait."

Music for Chameleons. New York: Random House, 1980.

B.   Stories (Uncollected)

"The Walls Are Cold," *Decade of Short Stories,* 4 (Fourth Quarter 1943): 27–30.

"A Mink of One's Own," *Decade of Short Stories,* 6 (Third Quarter 1944): 1–4.

"The Shape of Things," *Decade of Short Stories,* 6 (Fourth Quarter 1944): 21–23.

"Preacher's Legend," *Prairie Schooner,* 19 (Winter 1945): 265–274.

"Blind Items," *Ladies Home Journal,* January 1974, p. 81 ff.

"Mojave," *Esquire,* June 1975, pp. 83–91.

"La Côte Basque," *Esquire,* November 1975, pp. 110–19.

"Unspoiled Monsters," *Esquire,* May 1976, pp. 55–68.

"Kate McCloud," *Esquire,* December 1976, pp. 82–96.

"Dazzle," *Vogue,* December 1979, pp. 30–34.

C.   Nonfiction (Uncollected)

"This Winter's Mask," *Harper's Bazaar,* December 1947, pp. 100–105, 195–96.

"A House in Sicily," *Harper's Bazaar,* January 1951, pp. 153–55.

"La Divine," *Harper's Bazaar,* April 1952, pp. 148–49.

"The $6 Misunderstanding," *New York Review of Books,* 1, No. 2 (1963): 14.

"Plisetskaya: 'A Two-Headed Calf,' " *Vogue,* April 1964, p. 169.

"A Curious Gift," *Redbook,* June 1965, pp. 52–53, 92–94.

"The 'Sylvia' Odyssey," *Vogue,* January 1966, pp. 68–75.

"Two Faces and . . . a Landscape . . . ," *Vogue,* February 1966, pp. 144–49.

"Oliver Smith." In Roddy McDowell, *Double Exposure.* New York: Delacorte Press, 1966, pp. 152–53.

"Extreme Magic—An Awake Dream, Cruising up the Yugoslavian Coast," *Vogue,* April 1967, pp. 84–89, 146–47.

"Death Row, U.S.A.," *Esquire,* October 1968, pp. 194–196.

"Time, the Timeless and Beaton's Time Sequence," *Vogue,* November 1968, pp. 172–3.

"At the Sea and in the City," *House Beautiful,* April 1969, pp. 93–98.

"Donna Marella and the Avvocato," *Vogue,* April 1969, pp. 206–9.

"Elizabeth Taylor." *Ladies Home Journal,* December 1974, p. 72.

"Guests," *McCalls*, February 1977, pp. 132–137.

"Music for Chameleons," *The New Yorker*, 17 September 1979, pp. 126–131.

"Truman Capote," *Vogue*, December 1979, p. 260 ff.

II. BIOGRAPHICAL AND GENERAL CRITICISM

A. *Bibliographies and Checklists*

Bryer, Jackson R. "Truman Capote: A Bibliography." In *In Cold Blood: A Critical Handbook*. I. Malin, ed. Belmont, Cal.: Wadsworth Publishing Co., 1968.

Vanderwerken, David. "Truman Capote: 1943–1968. A Critical Bibliography." *Bulletin of Bibliography* 27 (1970): 57–60, 71.

Wall, Richard, and Carl Craycraft. "A Checklist of Works about Truman Capote." *Bulletin of the N. Y. Public Library* 71 (March 1967): 165–72.

B. *Books*

Aldridge, John. *After the Lost Generation: A Critical Study of the Writers of Two Wars*. New York: Noonday Press, 1958.

Allen, Walter. *The Modern Novel in Britain and the United States*. New York: E. P. Dutton, 1964.

Bradbury, John. *Renaissance in the South: A Critical History of the Literature, 1920–1960*. Chapel Hill: University of North Carolina Press, 1963.

Breit, Harvey. *The Writer Observed*. Cleveland: World, 1956.

Cowley, Malcolm. *The Literary Situation*. New York: Viking Press, 1954.

Eisinger, Chester. *Fiction of the Forties*. Chicago: University of Chicago Press, 1963.

Gordon, Caroline and Allen Tate. *The House of Fiction*. New York: Charles Scribner's, 1960.

Gossett, Louise. *Violence in Recent Southern Fiction*. Durham, N.C.: Duke University Press, 1965.

Hassan, Ihab. *Radical Innocence: The Contemporary American Novel*. Princeton, N.J.: Princeton University Press, 1961.

Hill, Patti. "Truman Capote." In *Writers at Work: The "Paris Review" Interviews*. Malcolm Cowley, ed. New York: Viking Press, 1959.

Kazin, Alfred. *Bright Book of Life*. Boston: Little, Brown, 1971; New York: Delta, 1974.

————. *Contemporaries*. Boston: Little, Brown, 1962.

————. *The Open Form: Essays For Our Time*. New York: Harcourt, Brace, and World, 1961.

Klein, Marcus. *After Alienation: American Novels in Mid-Century*. Cleveland: World, 1962.

Kunitz, Stanley, ed. *Twentieth Century Authors, First Supplement*. New York: H. W. Wilson, 1955.

Malin, Irving. *New American Gothic*. Carbondale: Southern Illinois University Press, 1962.

Nance, William. *The Worlds of Truman Capote*. New York: Stein and Day, 1970.

Newquist, Roy. *Counterpoint*. Chicago: Rand McNally, 1964.

Schorer, Mark. "McCullers and Capote: Basic Patterns." In *The Creative Present: Notes on Contemporary American Fiction*. Nona Balakian and Charles Simmons, eds. Garden City, N.Y.: Doubleday, 1963.

Sullivan, Walter, "The Continuing Renascence: Southern Fiction in the Fifties." In *South: Modern Southern Literature in Its Cultural Setting*. Louis Rubin and Robert Jacobs, eds. New York: Doubleday, 1961.

Waldmeir, Joseph, ed. *Recent American Fiction: Some Critical Views*. Boston: Houghton, Mifflin, 1963.

C. Articles in Periodicals

Aldridge, John. "America's Young Novelists: Uneasy Inheritors of a Revolution." *Saturday Review of Literature*, 12 February 1949, pp. 6–8, 36–37, 42.

Alexander, Shana. "A Nonfictional Visit with Truman Capote." *Life*, 18 February 1966, p. 22.

Balakian, Nona. "The Prophetic Vogue of the Anti-Heroine." *Southwest Review*, 47 (Spring 1962): 134–41.

Baldanza, Frank. "Plato in Dixie." *Georgia Review*, 12 (Summer 1958): 151–67.

Bucco, Martin. "Truman Capote and the Country below the Surface." *Four Quarters*, 7 (November 1957): 22–25.

Collins, Carvel. "Other Voices." *American Scholar*, 25 (Winter 1955–56): 108, 110, 112–16.

Fleming, Anne Taylor. "The Private World of Truman Capote." *New York Times Magazine*, 9 July 1978, pp. 22–25; 16 July 1978, pp. 12–15.

Hassan, Ihab. "Birth of a Heroine." *Prairie Schooner*, 34 (Spring 1960): 78–83.

Howard, Jane. "A Six-Year Literary Vigil." *Life*, 7 January 1966, pp. 70–72, 75–76.

Hyman, Stanley Edgar. "Some Trends in the Novel." *College English*, 20 (October 1958): 1–9.

Medwick, Cathleen. "Truman Capote: An Interview." *Vogue*, December 1979, p. 263 ff.

Mengeling, Marvin. "Other Voices, Other Rooms: Oedipus between the Covers." *American Imago*, 19 (Winter 1962): 361–74.

Moravia, Alberto. "Two American Writers." *Sewanee Review*, 68 (Summer 1960): 473–81.

Norden, Eric. "Interview: Truman Capote." *Playboy*, March 1968, pp. 51 ff.

O'Connor, William Van. "The Grotesque in Modern American Fiction." *College English*, 20 (April 1959): 342–46.

Rago, Henry. "The Discomforts of Storytelling." *Sewanee Review*, 56 (Summer 1948): 514–21.

Steinem, Gloria. "Go Right Ahead and Ask Me Anything." *McCalls*, November 1967, pp. 76–77.

Index

Aces Nelson, 178–80
Alice Lee Langman, 174, 182
Alter ego (double)
  in "Miriam," 39, 43, 44
  in "Shut a Final Door," 39
"Among the Paths to Eden," 8, 91, 106–10
Amy, 16, 20, 23
Angelita, 170
Anna Stimson, 34, 35, 38, 39, 182
Answered Prayers, 10–11, 165–83
  frame device in, 168, 170, 171
  homosexuality in, 166–67
  as rambling, 168
  sexuality in, 166–68
  in "Unspoiled Monsters," 177, 181
  see also "Côte Basque, La"; "Kate McCloud"; "Mojave"; "Unspoiled Monsters"
Appleseed, 60–61
Armstrong, Louis, 133, 135
Autobiographical elements
  in "A Christmas Memory," 97
  in *The Grass Harp,* 63
  in "Louis Armstrong," 135

in "New York," 113–15
in "Shut a Final Door," 181–82
in "The Thanksgiving Visitor," 103
in "Unspoiled Monsters," 172, 173, 175–77, 180–83
Autumn
  in *Breakfast at Tiffany's,* 87, 88
  in *The Grass Harp,* 69, 77
  See also Seasons
Avedon, Richard, 111, 132–34

Baby, 94–96
Barney, Natalie, 175
Beaton, Cecil, 181
Beat the Devil, 8
Bell, in *Other Voices, Other Rooms,* 17–18
Betrayal, in "The Headless Hawk," 46, 50
Billy Bob, 56, 57
Bird(s)
  in *In Cold Blood,* 162
  in "Lola," 138
  in "Shut a Final Door," 38
  in "To Europe," 120
"Blind Items," 166
Bobbit, Miss, 55–59, 79
Bogart, Humphrey, 133, 136

Bowles, Jane, 177
Brando, Marlon, 130–32
Breakfast at Tiffany's, 8, 79–89
  autumn in, 87, 88
  cat in, 86, 87
  "Children on Their Birthdays" and, 55
  critical response to, 79
  home in, 85–87
  lies in, 82–83
  living in the sky in, 58, 85–87
  love in, 83
  nostalgia in, 88
Breakfast at Tiffany's: A Short Novel and Three Short Stories, 91
Breen, Mrs., 126
Breen, Robert, 126
Brooklyn, in "A House on the Heights," 139
"Brooklyn," 115–16
Buckskin, Flo, 159
Buddy
  in "A Christmas Memory," 98–102
  in "The Thanksgiving Visitor," 103–6
Butterflies
  in "The Headless Hawk," 48
  in "A Ride through Spain," 124

Capote, Joseph, 2–3
Capote, Truman
  cycles in development of, 7–8
  depression of, 9, 10
  drinking and drug problems of, 10, 11
  early life of, 1–5
  homosexuality of, 9–10

  See also Autobiographical elements
Carlos, 170
Cat, in *Breakfast at Tiffany's*, 86, 87
Catherine, 64–70, 72, 75, 98, 99
"Cecil Beaton," 130
Cerf, Bennett, 141
Cerf, Christopher, 167
Chase, Richard, 7
Childhood, return to (regression), 44
  in "Master Misery," 32–33
Childhood terrors, 28
  in "Master Misery," 32
  in "A Tree of Night," 53
"Children on Their Birthdays," 28, 54, 59, 61
"Christmas Memory, A," 2, 3, 7, 8, 91, 97–103
  "The Thanksgiving Visitor" compared to, 103, 105, 106
Circularity
  in "Children on Their Birthdays," 55
  in *The Grass Harp*, 77
  in "The Headless Hawk," 44, 50
  in "Shut a Final Door," 33–34
Clift, Montgomery, 178–80
Clutter, Beverly, 145, 152
Clutter, Bonnie, 144, 145–47, 149, 150, 155
Clutter, Herbert, 141, 144–47, 150, 151, 153, 155
Clutter, Kenyon, 145, 147, 149–50
Clutter, Nancy, 144–47, 157
Cocteau, Jean, 134, 136, 175–76

Colette, 175–77
Collin Fewick, 63–70, 72–
    74, 76, 77, 79, 98, 99,
    102
Colors, see Green; Pink
Comedy, see Humor
Cooper, Gloria Vanderbilt,
    171
"Côte Basque, La," 166,
    170–72
Cruelty (malice), in "Shut
    a Final Door," 34, 37–
    38

Dad Henderson, 104
"Dazzle," 11, 183–85
Death
    in "A Christmas Mem-
        ory," 102
    in Other Voices, Other
        Rooms, 14–15, 19, 23–
        25
    in "A Tree of Night," 53–
        54
Denny Fouts, 174–75
Depression, Capote's, 9, 10
Destronelli, 46, 49
Destructiveness
    in "The Headless Hawk,"
        45, 47–50
    in "Shut a Final Door,"
        34, 35
Dewey, Alvin, 151, 152,
    154, 155, 164
"Diamond Guitar, A," 91–
    94
Dinesen, Isak, 134–35
D. J., 44–50
Doc Golightly, 80, 83–85
Dogs Bark, The, 10, 111,
    130, 134, 137–38
Dolly, Talbo, 64–77, 98, 99,
    102, 103
Double (alter ego)

in "Miriam," 39, 43, 44
    in "Shut a Final Door,"
        39
Dream(s)
    in "The Headless Hawk,"
        47–48
    in "Master Misery," 29,
        32
    in "Miriam," 41, 42
    in "Shut a Final Door,"
        38–39
Dreams, lost, in "New York,"
    113, 114
Drowning, in Other Voices,
    Other Rooms, 15, 20
"Duke in His Domain, The,"
    130–32
Dunphy, Jack, 10

Ed Sansom, 15, 16
Ellen, Aunt, 14, 15, 20, 24
Esquire (magazine), 11, 100
Estelle, 28–29
Esther Jackson, 108, 109
Europe, 120–21
"Ezra Pound," 136–37

Fall, see Autumn
Fame
    in "Children on Their
        Birthdays," 57
    in "Jug of Silver," 61
Father, search for a, in
    Other Voices, Other
    Rooms, 5, 15
Faulk, Sook, 2, 63, 97
    as character in "The
        Thanksgiving Visitor,"
        103–6
Femininity, in Other Voices,
    Other Rooms, 22
Ferguson, Mrs., 184–85
Film technique, in In Cold
    Blood, 143, 144

First-person narrative, 27
Fitzgerald, F. Scott, 11
Flowers, in "Among the Paths to Eden," 107, 109
"Fontana Vecchia," 137, 138
Frame device, in *Answered Prayers,* 168, 170, 171
Frost, Robert, 3

Garbo, Greta, 113
George Schmidt, 169–70
George Whitelaw, 169
Gershwin, Lee, 127
Gide, André, 134, 136, 185
Glass House, The, 91
God, in "A Christmas Memory," 101–2
Gossip, in "Shut a Final Door" and "Unspoiled Monsters," 182
Gossip columnists, 166
Gothicism, 2, 13–14, 17–18
   in *Other Voices, Other Rooms,* 5
Grass, in *The Grass Harp,* 102
Grass Harp, The, 2, 7, 63–77
   "Children on Their Birthdays" and, 55, 56
   "A Christmas Memory" compared to, 97–99, 102–3
   dramatic adaptation of, 77
   dropsy remedy invented by Dolly in, 65, 68–69
   grass in, 102
   grass harp in, 77
   humor in, 70–72
   innocence in, 63, 64, 67
   love in, 73–76
   pink in, 67
   religion in, 70, 71

revivalists in, 71–72
rooms of the house in, 67–68
societal rules in, 63, 65, 70, 72
"The Thanksgiving Visitor" compared to, 105
tree-house episodes in, 69–76
"Greek Paragraphs," 138, 139
Green
   in "The Headless Hawk," 49, 50
   in "Shut a Final Door," 37–38
   in "A Tree of Night," 51, 54
Grotesque characters (freaks)
   in "The Headless Hawk," 45
   in *Other Voices, Other Rooms,* 14–17
   in "A Tree of Night," 51
Guilt
   in "The Headless Hawk," 48
   in "Shut a Final Door," 37

Haha Jones, 99–100
"Haiti," 118–20
Hamlet, 152–53
Hamurabi, 60, 61
"Handcarved Coffins," 185, 186
Harry McCloud, 178
"Headless Hawk, The," 28, 44–50
Helm, Paul, 146, 147
Hemingway, Ernest, 11
Henry, 28–29
Hickock, Richard Eugene

(Dick), 145, 147–58, 160–63
arrest of, 155
Capote's attitude toward, 157–58
on Death Row, 157
early life of, 158
in Mexico, 151–53
planning of crime by, 148, 153
sexuality and, 161–62
trial of, 156–57
Hilary, 114
Hilcomb (Kansas), 145
Holly Golightly, 55, 58, 79–88
"Hollywood," 116–18, 165
Home, in *Breakfast at Tiffany's*, 85–87
Homosexuality
in *Answered Prayers*, 166 67
Capote's, 9–10
In *In Cold Blood*, 161–62
in *Other Voices, Other Rooms*, 5
in "Shut a Final Door," 37, 38
in "Unspoiled Monsters," 172–73, 180, 182
"House of Flowers, A," 7, 91, 94–97, 118–19
musical-comedy adaptation of, 97
"House on the Heights, A," 138, 139
Hulga, 169–70, 173
Humor (comedy)
in "Among the Paths to Eden," 106
in "A Christmas Memory," 99–100
in *The Grass Harp*, 70–72

in *The Muses Are Heard*, 125–28
"Humphrey Bogart," 136
Hutton, Barbara, 177–78
Hyppolite, 118

Idabel, 4, 16, 20–23
Immortality, in "Among the Paths to Eden," 108, 110
Ina Coolbirth, 171–72
In Cold Blood, 1, 6, 91, 132, 140–64
critical response to, 142, 143
film technique in, 143, 144
homosexuality in, 161–62
as nonfiction novel, 8–9, 143
Part I ("The Last to See Them Alive"), 145 50
Part II ("Persons Unknown"), 150–53
Part III ("Answer"), 153–56
Part IV ("The Corner"), 156–64
preparation for writing, 141 43
structure of, 144
See also Hickock, Richard Eugene; Smith, Perry Edward
Innocence, in *The Grass Harp*, 63, 64, 67
Innocents, The, 8
Irving, 34, 37
"Isak Dinesen," 134–35
"Ischia," 121–23
Isherwood, Christopher, 174
Isolation (solitude)
in "Miriam," 39–41, 43
See also Loneliness

Ivor Belli, 106–10
Ivory Hunter, 169–70

Jaime, 170
Jamison, 94–96
"Jane Bowles," 130
"Jean Cocteau and André
    Gide," 136
Jesus Fever, 16
Joe Bell, 81, 85, 88
Joel Knox Sansom, 14–25,
    64, 79
Jonquils, in "Among the
    Paths to Eden," 107
José, 83–85
Journalism, 8, 143
Judge Cool, 70–75, 77
"Jug of Silver," 28, 59–61

Kate McCloud, 174
    in "Unspoiled Monsters,"
    178
"Kate McCloud," 166, 178–
    80
Kay, 50–54
Keats, John, 121
Kennedy, John F., 174
Kidwell, Susan, 149, 164
Kurt Kuhnhardt, 34, 38, 39,
    182

Ladies Home Journal, 166
Lady Coolbirth, 171–72
Lazarus, story of, in "A
    Tree of Night," 52–54
Lee, Harper, 2, 4, 141–42
Lies (fabrications), in Break-
    fast at Tiffany's, 82–83
Life (magazine), 5–6
Lilacs, 54
Little Homer Honey, 71
Little Sunshine, 16, 20
Local Color, 7–8, 111–24,
    165
"Lola," 137, 138

Loneliness
    in New York, 113
    in Other Voices, Other
        Rooms, 19–21, 24
    See also Isolation
Los Angeles, 116–18
"Louis Armstrong," 135
Love
    in Breakfast at Tiffany's,
        83
    in The Grass Harp, 73–76
    in "House of Flowers," 95
    in "Mojave," 170
Lydia, Miss (Russian offi-
    cial), 127
Lyons, Leonard, 127

McCain, James, 141
McCullers, Carson, 170
Madness (psychosis)
    in "The Headless Hawk,"
        47–48
    See also Schizophrenia
"Mae West," 135
Mag Wildwood, 83
Mailer, Norman, 8
Malice (cruelty), in "Shut
    a Final Door," 34, 37–
    38
Manny Fox, 57
Margaret, 34, 37–39
"Marilyn Monroe," 137
Marshall, Mr., 59–61
Mary O'Meaghan, 107, 109
Masculinity (virility), in
    Other Voices, Other
    Rooms, 20–22
"Master Misery," 28–33, 44
Matthau, Mrs. Walter, 171
Maude Riordan, 73
Middy, 60–61
Miller, Arthur, 137
Miller, Mrs., 39, 43
Miriam, 40–43

"Miriam," 3, 39, 44, 180

"Mojave," 166, 168–70, 178

Molly Henderson, 104

Money, in "A Christmas Memory," 71–72, 99, 100

Monroe, Marilyn, 133, 137

Morgan, Helen, 108

Morris Ritz, Dr., 69, 75

Mortality, in "Among the Paths of Eden," 107, 110

Mozart, Miss, 29

Muses Are Heard, The, 8, 124–30

"Music for Chameleons," 165

Music for Chameleons, 11, 185

Mussolini family, 122

"My Side of the Matter," 28, 61, 62

Narcissism, in "Shut a Final Door," 33

Nature, in "A Christmas Memory," 101

Ned, 172

New Orleans, 4

"New Orleans," 111, 113

"New York," 113–15

New Yorker, The, 3–4, 8, 124, 165

Nonfiction novel, genre of, 8–9, 143

Nostalgia
  in *Breakfast at Tiffany's,* 88
  in "A Christmas Memory," 97, 102

Nye, Harold, 154

Observations, 7–8, 111, 132–37

O'Connor, Flannery, 173

Odd Henderson, 103–5

O'Henry Prize, 3

O. J. Berman, 82, 86

Old Bonaparte, 95–96

Orchids, in "Among the Path to Eden," 108, 109

Oreilly, 30–32

Orphan figure(s), 56
  in *Breakfast at Tiffany's,* 80
  in *The Grass Harp,* 64
  in *Other Voices, Other Rooms,* 64
  See also Father, search for a

Other Voices, Other Rooms, 4–7, 13–25, 54, 57, 64
  bell in, 17–18
  critical response to, 13
  death in, 14–15, 19, 23–25
  drowning in, 15, 20
  femininity in, 22
  gothicism in, 5
  grotesque characters in, 14–17
  homosexuality in, 5
  loneliness in, 19–21, 24
  masculinity in, 20–22
  models for Randolph in, 4–5
  photographs of Capote on book jacket of, 6, 181
  search for a father in, 5, 15
  snake in, 22
  sword in, 21–22

Ottilie, 94–97

P. B. Jones (Jonesy), 168, 170–83

Persephone myth, 54
Persons, Joseph, 2, 5
Persons, Nina, 2–3
Photograph(s)
    of Capote on book jacket
        of *Other Voices, Other
        Rooms,* 6, 181
    in *Local Color,* 111, 115,
        116, 118, 120–23
    in *Observations,* 132–37
Pink in *The Grass Harp,* 67
Pope, Alexander, 100
Porgy and Bess, 124–27,
    129–30
Pound, Ezra, 133, 136–37
Prison, in "A Diamond Gui-
    tar," 91
Prostitute(s)
    in "Haiti," 118–19
    in "Unspoiled Monsters,"
        178
Psychosis (madness)
    in "The Headless Hawk,"
        47–48
    See also Schizophrenia
Publicity (public relations),
    5–6

Queenie, 98, 99, 104

Rain, in "Children on Their
    Birthdays," 59
Randolph, Cousin, 4–5, 18–
    20, 23–25
Randolph Lee, 16
Random House, 3–4, 185
Religion
    in "Children on Their
        Birthdays," 57
    in *The Grass Harp,* 70,
        71
    in "A Christmas Mem-
        ory," 101–2

Revercomb, 29–32
Reverend Mr. Buster, 70
Revivalists   (evangelicals),
    in *The Grass Harp,* 71–
    72
"Ride through Spain, A,"
    123–24
Riley Henderson, 70–74
Romance, 7
Rome (Italy), 138
Rosa Cooper, 34, 35, 38, 39
Rosalba Cat, 56
Rosita, 94–96
Ross, Harold, 3
Royal Bonaparte, 94–97
Rupp, Bobby, 146, 147
Russia, 124–30
Rusty Trawler, 83

Sally Tomato, 80–81
Sarah, 168–70
Satire, in *The Muses Are
    Heard,* 126–27
Schaeffer, 92–94
Schizophrenia
    in "Miriam," 43
    See also Madness
Seasons
    in "Children on Their
        Birthdays," 58–59
    in "Fontana Vecchia,"
        139
    See also Autumn; Sum-
        mer
Selected Writings, 28, 130
Selma, 114–15
Sexuality
    in *Answered Prayers,*
        166–68
    in "Children on Their
        Birthdays," 56–57
    in "Kate McCloud," 179–
        80

in "Mojave," 169, 170
in "Unspoiled Monsters,"
   174, 175
See also Homosexuality
Sheriff Candle, 70, 72
Shotgun, 113
"Shut a Final Door," 33–39,
   44, 181–83
Sicily, 138
Sister Ida, 71–72
Sky, living in the
   in *Breakfast at Tiffany's,*
      58, 85–87
   in "Children on Their
      Birthdays," 58
Smith, Perry Edward, 142–
   45, 147–63
   arrest of, 155
   Capote's sympathy for,
      157, 163
   confession of, 155
   on Death Row, 157, 158
   early life of, 158–60, 162,
      163
   in Mexico, 151–53
   planning of crime by, 148,
      153
   psychological view of, 163
   sexuality and, 161–62
   trial of, 156–57
Smith, Tex John, 159–60
Snake, in *Other Voices,
   Other Rooms,* 22
Societal rules (or values),
   in *The Grass Harp,* 63,
   65, 70, 72
Solitude (isolation)
   in "Miriam," 39–41, 43
   See also Loneliness
Spain, 123–24
Stoecklein, Alfred, 145–46
Strange Dents, 11
Summer
   in "Children on Their

Birthdays," 58, 59
   See also Seasons
Summer Crossing, 4
Superstition, in "A Christ-
   mas Memory," 100
Sword, in *Other Voices,
   Other Rooms,* 21–22
Sylvester, 62
Sylvia, 28–33

"Tangier," 123
Taormina (Italy), 138
"Thanksgiving Visitor,
   The," 2, 8
Third-person narrative, 27
Tico Feo, 92–93
"To Europe," 120–21
Toklas, Alice B., 175
"Tree of Night, A," 44, 50–
   54
   female and male charac-
      ters in, 44
*Tree of Night and Other
   Stories, A,* 7, 27–62
   dark stories, 27–54
   order of stories in, 28
   sunlight stories, 27, 28,
      54–62
Turner Boatwright (Boaty),
   173–74, 179, 182

Uncle B., 105–6
"Unspoiled Monsters," 166,
   172–78, 180, 183

Verena Talbo, 64–69
Vidal, Gore, 174
Vincent, 44–50
Virility (masculinity), in
   *Other Voices, Other
   Rooms,* 20–22
Vitale, Joe, 114

Vogue (magazine), 6, 167
Voodoo ceremony, in "Haiti," 119–20

Walter Ranney, 33–39, 181–83
Watson, Warner, 126–27, 129
Wells, Floyd, 153–54
West, Mae, 134

"White Rose, The," 175–77
Willie-Jay, 148, 159
Wisteria, Miss, 16, 23
Witchcraft, in "Jug of Silver," 60–61
Womb images, in "Shut a Final Door," 37
Wood, Catharine, 3

Zoo, 16, 20, 21, 24

MODERN LITERATURE SERIES

In the same series (continued from page ii)

ANDRÉ MALRAUX   *James Robert Hewitt*
THOMAS MANN   *Arnold Bauer*
CARSON MCCULLERS   *Richard M. Cook*
ALBERTO MORAVIA   *Jane E. Cottrell*
VLADIMIR NABOKOV   *Donald E. Morton*
ANAÏS NIN   *Bettina L. Knapp*
JOYCE CAROL OATES   *Ellen G. Friedman*
FLANNERY O'CONNOR   *Dorothy Tuck McFarland*
EUGENE O'NEILL   *Horst Frenz*
JOSÉ ORTEGA Y GASSET   *Franz Niedermayer*
GEORGE ORWELL   *Robert Kalechofsky*
KATHERINE ANNE PORTER   *John Edward Hardy*
EZRA POUND   *Jeannette Lander*
MARCEL PROUST   *James R. Hewitt*
RAINER MARIA RILKE   *Arnold Bauer*
J. D. SALINGER   *James Lundquist*
UPTON SINCLAIR   *Jon Yoder*
ISAAC BASHEVIS SINGER   *Irving Malin*
LINCOLN STEFFENS   *Robert Stinson*
JOHN STEINBECK   *Paul McCarthy*
JOHN UPDIKE   *Suzanne Henning Uphaus*
KURT VONNEGUT   *James Lundquist*
PETER WEISS   *Otto F. Best*
EDITH WHARTON   *Richard H. Lawson*
THORNTON WILDER   *Hermann Stresau*
THOMAS WOLFE   *Fritz Heinrich Ryssel*
VIRGINIA WOOLF   *Manly Johnson*
RICHARD WRIGHT   *David Bakish*
EMILE ZOLA   *Betlina L. Knapp*
CARL ZUCKMAYER   *Arnold Bauer*